STUDIA ROMANICA
Band 215

Herausgegeben von
Marc Föcking
Robert Folger
Sybille Große
Edgar Radtke

GERHARD POPPENBERG

The Antinomy of the Law

The Myth of Orestes in Antiquity and Modernity

Translated from the German
by
MARK HEWSON

Universitätsverlag
WINTER
Heidelberg

Bibliografische Information der Deutschen Nationalbibliothek

Die Deutsche Nationalbibliothek verzeichnet diese Publikation
in der Deutschen Nationalbibliografie;
detaillierte bibliografische Daten sind im Internet
über *http://dnb.d-nb.de* abrufbar.

Gerhard Poppenberg:
Die Antinomie des Gesetzes. Der Orest-Mythos in der Antike und der Moderne

UMSCHLAGBILD

Das Titelbild zeigt die Szene vor dem Muttermord des Orest in Peter Steins Inszenierung der *Orestie* des Aischylos an der Berliner Schaubühne am Lehniner Platz im Jahr 1980 mit Udo Samel in der Rolle des Orest und Edith Clever in der Rolle der Klytaimestra. Photo: © ruth walz

Halt ein, o Sohn! Und hege Scheu vor ihr, mein Kind,
Der Brust, an der du oft ja schlummernd lagst zugleich
Zahnlosen Mündchens saugtest süßernährende Milch!

Die Weihgussträgerinnen V. 896–898 (Übersetzer: Oskar Werner)

ISBN 978-3-8253-6911-8

Imprimé en Allemagne · Printed in Germany
Druck: Memminger MedienCentrum, 87700 Memmingen

Gedruckt auf umweltfreundlichem, chlorfrei gebleichtem
und alterungsbeständigem Papier.

Den Verlag erreichen Sie im Internet unter:
www.winter-verlag.de

La folie ne fait pas droit
Jean-Jacques Rousseau: *Du contrat social*

Table of contents

zation of the camps, humanization of extermination – “to have stayed decent”: Auschwitz as legal space – the words of the Führer, legal force and the categorical imperative – Kant: *Groundwork to the Metaphysics of Morals* – reason and humanity as instance of the law – *petitio principii* of freedom, humanity and law – lawfulness of the extermination of the enemy – people and race as instance of the law – Arendt: *Eichmann in Jerusalem* – “fearsome banality” and *hostis generis humani* – ethos of apathy – collapse of father-image and fatherland – wish, reality, phantasma – psychaesthenia, delusions of grandeur, dissolution of limits – the nameless.

5 Psychosis

The end of the war as collapse – Freud and Schreber – delusion and transformation – black pedagogy – Lacan and Schreber – the Oedipus complex as the foundation of the symbolic order – family romance and sexual difference – the navel of the dream and of the symbolic order – Orestes and Oedipus – Aeschylus: *Oresteia* – the order of the mother and the law of the father – the navel of the earth – true and delusive order.

1 Mythos

But what if the City were a growing neoplasm,
across the centuries, always changing
to meet exactly the changing shape
of its very worst, secret fears?
Thomas Pynchon, *Gravity's Rainbow*

With the epic and the drama, ancient Greek civilization developed a symbolic form with a long-term effect that continues up to the present day: literature. With the drama this form showed its power in the public space of the *polis* to the highest degree. Greek drama put the histories of individual families on the stage. Since the families in question are those of the rulers, these family-dramas are at the same time also political dramas. For this reason, the dramatically represented stories of the families – the myths of the tragedies – are also elements of the political constitution of society. The myths function to articulate the order of both the private and domestic sphere and the public and political sphere – above all, because violence is elementary and constitutive in both domains. In the myths the violence of the family is configured with the violence of the community. Violence governs the relations within families and between families. These agonistic relations form a nexus of violence which is the origin of the community formed around such family bonds.

In the *Poetics*, Aristotle discusses the mythical articulation of *oikos* and *polis*, familial and social order in the medium of *pathos*. The drama politicizes and socializes the economy of individual feeling. The drives and affects of the individual are configured by the myths with a view to the element of universality that governs the polis. The elementary political significance of the mythic narratives is to be located at this point. They give the community and its political order a constitution for the affects, and in this way, they shape the affect-structure of the political. They represent social relations such as they exist at a given moment, and provide them with a symbolic expression: as such, they have a performative aspect, in that they also create and shape this existing order. The myths are a configuration of the economy of the affects: they give an expression to feelings, but they also shape and form them. They furnish the elements of a political pathology, making possible a description and a study of the general state of the feelings.

Sigmund Freud understood the correspondence of *pathos* and *mythos* as a fundamental element of psychoanalysis. In a letter to Wilhelm Fliess (12.12.1897), he reports his discovery that the "endopsychic myths" of the drive-structure are "projected outwards" in the form of mythic configurations: he names this "psychomythology".[1] In

[1] Sigmund Freud: *The Origins of Psychoanalysis. Letters to Wilhelm Flies. Drafts and Notes 1887-1902*. translated by Eric Mosbacher and James Strachey. London: Imago, 1954, p. 237.

"Creative Writers and Day-Dreaming" (1907) he speaks of myths as the "wishful fantasies of whole nations, the secular dreams of youthful humanity".[2] And in the thirty-second of the *Introductory Lectures on Psychoanalysis* (1933), he introduces his discussion of the "the life of the instincts" with the claim that "the theory of the instincts is so to say our mythology". The structure of the instincts is formed out of two conflicting drives, which Freud conceives first as the sexual drive and the ego-drive, later as *Eros* and *Thanatos*, life-drive and death-drive. *Eros* is the progressive drive towards union with others, towards the "synthesis of living things into greater unities". *Thanatos* is the regressive drive, back towards a condition of inertia, and in the end, towards inorganic existence. It is characteristic of both that they can be satisfied by proxies and substitutes, by an alternative object or alternative means. By the same token, this means that the dynamics and the economy of substitution, of representation and of metaphorical configuration originate from this instinctive energy. The life of the drives is the deep-structure of the metaphorical capacity.

The satisfaction of *Eros* is inhibited by the reality principle, in the sense of the totality of the demands made by the exterior world and by civilization. This is the principle that demands substitutive representation in order to satisfy the sexual drives through other real, phantasmatic or ideal objects. The drives to life and self-preservation block the satisfaction of the death drive, which pushes toward self-destruction. This latter drive also requires a substitution; the "tendency to self-destruction" is projected outwards, in the form of aggression. "It really seems as though it is necessary for us to destroy some other thing or person in order not to destroy ourselves".[3] The structure of substitution is therefore essential to the drives, the basis of life as such, given from the beginning with their conflictual constitution. *Eros* is the agent of conversion and replacement by which the death-drive is projected outwards. And this "outside" is the agent of the re-orientation and replacement that sublimates *Eros* into other objects. *Eros* and *Thanatos* are mythical figures serving to conceptualize the structure of the drives. Their fundamental agon is "our mythology". The myths provide the materials for a "mytho-psychology". At the same time, these mythic figures allow us to recognize the principle of myth-formation in the projection of the drive-structure. The result is the external world, configured in the mode of a civilization. The myths, these "secular dreams of youthful humanity", are a symbolic form of this projection; they allow us to see that the process of civilization *forms* the mythos of humanity.

The family-drama of the Atreides gives rise to a mythic complex that reveals its power over a *longue durée*. It is one of the myths of origin of Greek civilization, and it is bound up with the beginnings of the political order on the Peloponnese. The pre-history of the Atreides begins with Tantalus, the son of Zeus. He was a guest at Olympus, where he stole the meal of the gods, Ambrosia, in order to share it with the humans, with whom, moreover, he also shared the secrets of the gods. Then, at a meal

2 Sigmund Freud: *Creative Writers and Daydreaming* (1908), in: *The Standard Edition of the Complete Psychological Works of Sigmund Freud, Vol IX (1906-1908) Jensen's Gradiva and other works*, p. 149.

3 Sigmund Freud: *New Introductory Lectures on Psychoanalysis* (1933), in: *The Standard Edition of the Complete Psychological Works of Sigmund Freud, Vol XX (1932-1936): New Introductory Lectures on Psychoanalysis and other works*, p. 95, p. 107, 104.

which he prepared for the Olympians, he served them his own dismembered and cooked son, Pelops, as a meal. The agonistic relationship between father and son is repeated in the subsequent generations.

The gods discover the crime of Tantalus, and Pelops is put back together and brought back to life by Zeus. He then becomes the lord of a large area of land, which he names the Peloponnese, the Island of Pelops. The sceptre of the empire of Greece passes through his sons to Agamemnon, the father of Orestes. The myth of Orestes forms a conclusion to a family history marked by hate and violence, which is at the same time the primeval history of political power and dominance in Greece. In this way, myth gives a deep-structure to the political. The sons of Pelops, Atreus and Thyestes, having killed their brother Chrysippos, also have an antagonistic relationship. Through a ruse, Thyestes brings it about that Atreus kills his own son; to revenge himself Atreus presents his brother with his own children, slaughtered and killed, as a meal. The curse on the race of Tantalus continues in the following generations. At the end of the first part of Aeschylus' *Oresteia*, the Chorus sums up the family history: "The race is bound fast in calamity".[4] Agamemnon, the son of Atreus, sacrifices his daughter Iphigenia, in order to atone for having offended the goddess Artemis, and so to end the lull in the wind which stops the Greek fleet from sailing to Troy. The Trojan War also takes place within the horizon of the myth of the Atreides; it begins because the Trojan prince Paris has run off with Helen, the wife of Menelaus, from Atreus' other son. Clytemnestra, the wife of Agamemnon, kills her husband after his return from war, as revenge for her daughter's death. This in turn leads Orestes, the son of Agamemnon and Clytemnestra, to avenge his father by killing his mother and her lover, Aegisthus, a son of Thyestes.

The disaster that befalls the family has its origins in the violence between the generations. The parents kill the children, and eat them, or serve them to be eaten; the children kill the parents. The violence stems above all from the fathers. The special relationship of Tantalus to the Olympian gods reminds us that the genealogy of the gods too, from Uranus to Kronos to Zeus, is a sequence of generational conflicts, made up of hatred and violence, struggle and murder. Uranus banishes his children, the Titans, to Tartarus. His son Kronos emasculates him, and takes over the leadership, and then attempts to secure it by eating his children, until his own son Zeus emasculates him in turn and takes over the leadership of Olympus. The apparatus of the gods and the Olympian order that stands over human society is founded upon a sequence of familial acts of violence. Their history is a mythic projection of human history. Correspondingly, the myth of the Atreides also deals with violence as the agency of Greek history. And this violence again has its deep structure in family relationships. The *mythos* of the family provides the paradigm for the order of the *polis*, and the political, and the mythic genealogy of the gods provides its meta-myth.

The Greek myths have been subject to continual literary re-workings, first by the Greeks themselves, then by the Romans, and then, ever again, over the next two thousand years, up until the present. "A lot of situations repeat themselves, no doubt about it. They recur: yesterday, today, a long time ago. They come back, they come from the dawn of time, it's happened once, ten times, and in spite of changes of detail, it's

4 *Agamemnon*, v. 1566: in: Aeschylus: *Oresteia*, translated by Herbert Weir Smyth, Loeb, 1926.

always the same event. Don't you find that strange?" (MH, 87). If mythically configured literature was the form of *pathos* in the public sphere of Greek civilization, one can assume that the subsequent revisions of these myths have served a corresponding function. The myths of the Greeks, then, would have a general significance, which would extend beyond the domain of their own civilization, to the extent that this civilization has provided the determining model for Western history; this general significance is historical, the myths have become part of the Western symbolic system.

Literary works come back to the myths in order to re-deploy their potential to give structure and to channel and configure affects – that is their signifying power. Significance is an *effect* that the myth has, which makes it into something real, active. The myth realizes itself ever anew, in shaping and configuring new material in accordance with its own structure. And in the various realizations of the myth, its diverse dimensions unfold, just as a concept unfolds in the course of its conceptual history, or a theoretical problem unfolds in the course of its discursive history.

With the title of his novel, *Les Bienveillantes*, Jonathan Littell explicitly refers back to the third part of the *Oresteia* (*The Eumenides*), and encouraged his translators to use the version of the Aeschylean drama current in their own language for the title of the book. The English translator Charlotte Mandell chose *The Kindly Ones*. In a conversation with Littell, the historian Pierre Nora sought to encapsulate what was most characteristic about the novel. For Nora, Littell writes "with literary means about the execution, about the murder itself, the blind spot which historians had bracketed and could not directly access".This perspective, however, would make the novel into an illustrative supplement to the historiographical report. Littell, to the contrary, had made it clear that his interests lay elsewhere; he was first able to write the novel, he recounts, when he found the "fundamental structure" in the Orestes myth. The fictional re-working of the documentary material aims at more than mere illustration. The novel gives a literary form to the history of German fascism, of the Second World War and the extermination of the European Jews in order to explore not "the truth", but certainly "a truth" of history, and to "approach truth in a different way", than the historians do.[5] The mythical structure gives the facts meaning.

The protagonist of the novel, Max Aue, becomes an emblematic figure of the fascists, one who, perhaps – like the *condottiere* for the Renaissance or the *philosophe* for the Enlightenment – can stand as a figure for modernity. Littell develops the character's drive- and affect-structure, his "family-romance" (Freud), his relation to his mother and his father, his stepfather and his sister, after the myth of Orestes, which thus is intended to give an essential insight into the make-up of fascism; this is the central conceit of the novel. The objection, which has been raised at times, that Max Aue is not plausible, is not convincing, since the novel does not make a claim upon a referential realism. "It was not a matter of probability, for me", Littell said in conversation with Samuel Blumenfeld, "but of truth. You cannot create a novel if you insist solely on plausibility. Novelistic truth is a different thing from historic or sociological truth." The mythic structure of fiction in general and of the myth of Orestes in this particular case is the agent of this improbable truth.

[5] Jonathan Littell / Pierre Nora: *Conversation sur l'histoire et le roman*, in: *Le Débat* 144 (2007), p. 35-36, p. 30.

Already, in his novel *Le Très-Haut* (*The Most High*), written shortly after the war (1948), Maurice Blanchot had made the city struck by an epidemic into the vehicle for a literary representation of fascism.[6] The protagonist of this novel, too, is modelled after Orestes. Littell alludes to Blanchot: Max Aue reads his book *Faux Pas* (1943), a collection of literary-critical essays. In this collection Blanchot discusses Sartre's resistance drama, *Les Mouches* (*The Flies*, 1943), and in the process, reveals certain aporetic-antinomic structural moments in the Orestes myth – Sartre himself having treated the theme of the resistance against Fascism in the disguised form of a re-working of the Orestes narrative.

The reflections that follow will examine these three modern French versions of the Orestes myth in order to investigate the distinctive elements of this myth, how these elements were deployed in antiquity, and how the myth is re-made by the moderns. The question, ultimately, is how the Orestes myth is able to articulate the complex of motivations that are here at issue. The basic structure of the myth can be recognized in Aeschylus' *Oresteia*. Its pathological fringe – the madness in the mental state of Orestes – becomes more apparent in Euripides' *Orestes*. Blanchot accentuates this element. Henri Sorge, in *The Most High*, slips increasingly into psychosis: and in *The Kindly Ones*, too, Max Aue passes through a number of phases in which he seems to cross the boundary into madness. If, as has often been diagnosed, the breakdown of civilization of the 20th century signifies, beyond its own particular character, the collapse of the Western symbolic-system, then the collapse of the individual symbolic system in the madness of an individual has an emblematic value in just the measure that the particular individual can be seen as an incarnation of a more general predicament.

The Kindly Ones is written in the first person singular, as the autobiographical report of Max Aue.[7] In conversation with Pierre Nora, Littell made an intriguing remark, which allows one to see the uncanny way in which the border between author and the narrator can dissolve. The "I" of the narrator has for him the function of a "he", because the "he" is also more "I" than the "I". [...] I know that this very easily leads to misunderstandings, but I have taken myself as the model for this person. His worldview is not far from mine, even if I stand on the one side, and he stands on the other.[8] The narrative stance has an inherent tendency towards schizophrenia. The peculiar interference between "he" and "I" – which goes so far that Max Aue and Jonathan Littell share the same birthday (October 13), and Max Aue is circumcised (K, 199, 189) – enables Littell to reveal the other in the self, the brother Aue. The novel is accordingly addressed to "my human brothers" (K, 3, 11). At the end of the introductory chapter, "Toccata", Aue

6 Maurice Blanchot: *Le Très-Haut*, Paris, Gallimard, 1975 ([1]1948) / *The Most High*, translated by Allan Stoekl, Lincoln, University of Nebraska Press, 1996. This novel is cited in parentheses with the abbreviation (MH); the first number is referring to the English translation, and the second to the original French.

7 Jonathan Littell: *Les bienveillantes*, Paris, Gallimard, 2006 / *The Kindly Ones*, translated by Charlotte Mandell, London, Chatto and Windus, 2009. This novel is cited in parentheses with the abbreviation (K); the first number is referring to the English translation, and the second to the original French.

8 Jonathan Littell / Pierre Nora: *Conversation sur l'histoire et le roman*, in: *Le Débat* 144 (2007), p. 29.

says that he is a “man like any other”. “I am a man like you. I am like you” (K, 24, 30).[9] The basic operation of the novel, then, consists in the articulation of these two sides as dimensions of one mental state. The Jewish philosopher and political theologian, Jacob Taubes, who had a gift for illuminating historical constellations in astute formulations, sums up the point. “Many of us would gladly have participated, it was only that we were not allowed to”. Before Hannah Arendt, in her report on *Eichmann in Jerusalem*, noting that all Jews condemned the (*Gleichschaltungen*) of 1933, which excluded them “from one day to the next”, had also wondered: “Is it conceivable that none of them ever asked himself how many of his own group would have done just the same if only they had been allowed to?” (296) The question that follows – “is their condemnation today any the less correct for that reasons?” – makes it clear that such reflections do not imply a relativization of guilt, but give a glimpse into the uncanny structure of the judgment.

This could also explain the particular place of Maurice Blanchot in this complex. Blanchot, alongside Sartre, played an important and influential role in the post-war debates in literary theory in France.[10] A host of influential theorists of the 1960s and 1970s in France, among them Barthes, Deleuze, Derrida, Foucault, Lacan and Levinas, have their point of intersection in Blanchot and develop the figures of his thought. Subsequently in the 1970s and 1980s, in the USA, Blanchot’s trajectory – that of the author, not the man (the author function, in Foucault’s terms) – in the context of deconstructive literary criticism, elevated him to the status of a canonical reference for contemporary theory-formation.

In the immediate post-war period, Blanchot challenged Sartre’s call for the political engagement of the writer, marking out the claims of an *écriture pure*, a conception of literature and theory whose task consists in investigating its own condition of possibility, in order thus to provide a new foundation of thought and writing after the radical civilizational break imposed by the war and the Shoa. Motifs from Blanchot’s opposition to Sartre at the end of the 1940s reappear in the dissolution of the “Sartre-paradigm” at the beginning of the 1960s, starting with the concluding chapter of Lévi-

9 Martin von Koppenfels in his book *Schwarzer Peter. Der Fall Littell, die Leser und die Täter*, Göttingen, Wallstein, 2012 is concerned with the narrative position of the novel – which he names the “despicable narration” – and the position of the reader that it produces. He develops his study in the space of the concept of identification with the protagonist. In the case such as this, where the protagonist is a figure of evil and a despicable narrator, the result is strong resistance and conflict in the reader. Although von Koppenfels mentions that the question of identification is discussed at the very beginning of the novel, he scarcely reflects upon this fact. Max Aue addresses the readers as “human brothers” and identifies them with himself. This reverses the perspective and shifts the question of identification to another level. Our considerations here are oriented towards this level. They are concerned with the meaning of Littell’s novel and of the Orestes myth more generally. The recourse to the Oresteia of Aeschylus is not intended to demonize the National Socialists, nor to give the Nazi criminals a tragic aura, as Koppenfels consistently argues, but rather to explore a mythic condition – what one can call the Oresteian complex.

10 On this subject, see Andreas Gelhard: *Das Denken des Unmöglichen. Sprache, Tod und Inspiration in den Schriften Maurice Blanchots*, München, Fink, 2005 and Gerhard Poppenberg: *Ins Ungebundene. Über Literatur nach Blanchot*, Tübingen, Niemeyer, 1993.

Strauss' *The Savage Mind*. The theory-projections of the 1960s and 1970s and the debates that follow, even up until today, recognizably have their theoretical impetus and their generational configuration as responses to these discussions initiated immediately after the war. Their deepest core, too, lies with the complex for which "Auschwitz" has become established as the name.

The role played by Blanchot, the author, led to an interest in the person Blanchot, whose literary and theoretical writings began to appear from the beginning of the 1940s: texts of a man at that time nearly forty years old. The pre-history of the person seemed to collide with the author-function. In the 1920s and 1930s, Blanchot had been active as a political journalist in right-wing circles affiliated with the *Action Française*. This political background appeared strange and uncanny, since it did not seem to be compatible with the attitude of the altogether left-leaning stances of the Paris intelligentsia, or that of the American university-milieu, nor for that matter with Blanchot's own sympathies for the student rebellions of the 1960s. Was an entire intellectual generation somehow deceived, or did Blanchot, the person, pass through a radical change of position?[11]

It may be that conversion is precisely the figure that allows us to clarify the complex situation, since it is able to incorporate both sides of this alternative. In the case of Blanchot, we have someone who is at once a writer of editorials in the right-wing nationalist milieus of the 1930s, someone who had links to the Resistance in the 1940s, who saved the wife of his friend, the Jewish philosopher Emmanuel Levinas from deportation, who was proposed by Jean Paulhan as a replacement for Drieu la Rochelle, as editor of the NRF, who is an intellectual leader of the 1940s and 1950s, whose articles appear in the most prestigious journals and publishing houses – including the resistance publisher, Minuit – and finally also, a thinker whose work increasingly concentrates on the extermination of the Jews in the Nazi concentration camps. The identification of the political position of Blanchot is clearly a very difficult problem. Littell's statement that he himself was the "model" for Max Aue leads into the same set of questions. The encounter with the myth of Orestes will allow us to bring these questions into a somewhat clearer outline.

[11] See Jeffrey Mehlman: *Legacies of Anti-Semitism in France*, Minneapolis, University of Minnesota Press, 1983 and Steven Ungar: *Scandal & Aftereffect. Blanchot and France since 1930*, Minneapolis, University of Minnesota Press, 1995. On these debates, see Gerhard Poppenberg: *Mit Nachsicht?* in: *PhiN* 1 (1997), p. 69–72, Christophe Bident: *Blanchot – partenaire invisible. Essai biographique*, Paris, Champ Vallon, 1998, Giuseppina Mecchia: *L'écrivain et la communauté: Maurice Blanchot et la politique de 1932 à 1968*, Princeton, Princeton UP, 1997 and Hannes Opelz: *The Political Share of Literature. Maurice Blanchot*, 1931–1937, in: *Paragraph. Journal of Modern Critical Theory* 33 (2010) 1, p. 70–89 (with further literature).

2 Orestes

Pour la tenter, j'appelai doucement la loi:
"Approche, que je te voie face à face."
Maurice Blanchot: *La folie du jour*

The title of the novel *Le Très-Haut* (1948) is taken from an expression used in French as a paraphrase for God. The novel takes place in an unnamed city afflicted with an unspecified epidemic, perhaps plague, and largely concerns the efforts to deal with this outbreak. A year earlier, Camus had represented the occupation of France by the National Socialists through the allegory of a city struck with an epidemic. In Blanchot's novel, the epidemic functions as a figure for an authoritarian state.[12] The protagonist Henri Sorge embodies care (*die Sorge* in German) for the well-being of the collective, the state and the law, under conditions where these principles are endangered by the representatives of the state and the law themselves. Through this character, the novel exhibits the aporia of this care under the conditions of a general epidemic which, if not caused by the leadership of the state, is certainly exploited by it in order to install dictatorial structures. The result is the schizoid predicament where it becomes necessary to fight the law in order to preserve it, to break the law in order to maintain it. This fundamental antinomy drives Sorge into psychosis, in which he becomes himself "le Très-Haut", the "Most High". In his *Elements of the Philosophy of Right*, Hegel nominated the idea of the state as the "real God": "The state consists in the march of God in the world, and its basis is the power of reason actualizing itself as will" (§ 258).

In his 1966 essay on Blanchot, "The Thought of the Outside", Michel Foucault suggested that the novel *The Most High* should be read as a re-working of the myth of Orestes. "Sorge is Orestes in submission, an Orestes whose concern is to escape the law in order to fall further into submission to it."[13] Given that this re-casting of the Orestes myth takes place at the very moment that, in his theoretical work, Blanchot is in debate with Sartre and his concept of the political engagement of literature, it may be assumed

[12] Much later, in 1984, in a reflection on the status of the political, Blanchot writes that fascism had the "tendency" "to spread itself like an epidemic". See Maurice Blanchot: *The Intellectuals in Question*, in: *The Blanchot Reader*. Edited by Michael Holland. London: Blackwell, 1995/ *Les Intellectuels en Question: Ébauche d'une réflexion* in: *Le Débat* 29 (1984) and Paris, Fourbis, 1996., p. 220, 49.

[13] Michel Foucault and Maurice Blanchot: *Foucault / Blanchot.* Trans. Brian Massumi and Jeffrey Mehlman. Cambridge MA and New York, Zone Books, 1987, p. 39. Foucault here takes up a suggestion made by Robert Mantero and Bernard Pingaud in their presentation of Blanchot: "Sorge could be Orestes". See Robert Mantero / Bernard Pingaud: *Ecrivains d'aujourd'hui. 1940–1960*, Paris, Grasset, 1960, p. 104.

that *The Most High* also stands in a critical relation to Sartre – namely, to his own Orestes drama, *The Flies.*[14]

Sartre's play of 1943 was long seen as the Resistance drama *par excellence*; it contributed to founding and sustaining the myth of a Resistance literature after the war. Sartre did not stint in promoting this legend. In the preface to the German translation, he writes: "After our defeat in the year 1940, many Frenchmen gave in to despondency or allowed space for self-doubt within themselves. I, however, wrote *The Flies*." We know today that the reception of his contemporaries was far less enthusiastic than Sartre when he wrote it; hardly anyone had understood or wanted to understand the play in the sense he intended. The Resistance as a movement supported by a wide strata of society only began later – and certainly not under the impetus of such literary efforts. In any case, it is difficult to see how a drama directed at a large public could have been understood as a call for resistance, while at the same time escaping the attention of the German censors and the French collaborators. The notion of such an immediate intervention does not allow one to gauge the real complexity of the relation between literature and politics. Already in his text of 1943, Blanchot pointed towards the fundamental implications of this relationship, when he refers to the play as "the tragedy of liberation or freedom".

As a drama of freedom, Aeschylus' *Oresteia* is also a drama of power, of rule and of the law. The myth of Atreides interprets the pre-history of Greece as a series of struggles over power and the law, crime and malediction, guilt and expiation. The moving principle of history appears as the struggle for the law, and this contest is seen as an uninterrupted series of crimes: its center, perhaps even its truth, is an ineluctable guilt. Since the revenge and the expiation for a crime is itself a new crime, it perpetuates the guilt, which then demands punishment and expiation anew; thus the cycle of guilt and law continues. The right of revenge is always and at the same time also injustice, and the injustice that is committed is, at the same time, justified punishment. "Reproach thus meets reproach in turn / hard is the struggle to decide. / The spoiler is despoiled, the slayer pays penalty. / Yet, while Zeus remains on his throne, it remains true / that to him who does, it shall be done; for it is law. / Who can cast from out the house the seed of the curse? / The race is bound fast in calamity." (*Agamemnon*, v. 1560-1566).

The pre-history of the house of Atreus is the cause of the present events, which are the culmination of the history. In Aeschylus' dramatization, this history is given a poetic configuration, which allows one to see its meaning. The *Oresteia* shows the agonal ground of the family-history of the Atreides; and since their history is also the history of power in the *polis*, it shows the agonal ground of the state and its ordering by the law. In *Aischylos als Regisseur und Theologe* [*Aeschylus as Director and Theologian*] – sketched out in early 1945, published in 1949 – Karl Reinhardt speaks of the "collective responsibility of all members, whether those of a single family, or those of a whole polis". Martin Hose has analysed the *Oresteia* as a spiritual site of memory for antiquity. The play constitutes a memorial as a model of "political art" (Christian Meyer): it

[14] "One would say they are flies", the gardener in Giraudoux's *Elèctre* (1937) says of the Little Eumenides. Already in Aeschylus, Clytemnestra loses sleep due to mosquitoes (*Agamemnon*, v. 892). And in Blanchot's novel, there is a peculiar "Service des Mouches – a Fly-Department" (MH, 66, 69).

gives the *polis* its nomological knowledge in the medium of dramatic representation, and reveals the "decision dilemma" as the problematic meaning of this knowledge.

For this reason, Aeschylus structured the *Oresteia* as the struggle of two orders of law, two kinds of *Dike*: "Ares will encounter Ares; Right will encounter Right – *'Ares 'Arei xymbaleï, Díka Díka*" (*The Libation Bearers*, v. 461). These words of Orestes are the numerical and conceptual center of articulation of the trilogy, and constitute its meaning. Karl Reinhardt analyses this "conflict of orders" dramaturgically as the composition of "image and counter-image". What from one point of view is spouse-murder is from another point of view revenge for the murder of a daughter: what from one point of view is matricide is from another point of view revenge for the murder of the father. The dramaturgical symmetry corresponds to this situation. The murder of Agamemnon and Cassandra in *Agamemnon* correlates to the murder of Clytemnestra and Aegisthus in *The Libation Bearers*. The two parts each conclude with an opposing justification: Clytemnestra calls on the maternal order, Orestes on the paternal order. In the *Euminedes*, these opposed positions are taken up again during the negotiations in Delphi and Athens, and duplicated by the divine participants. Clytemnestra is represented by the Erinyes, Orestes by Apollo. This means that the maternal order is that of darkness and night – whose daughters are the Erinyes – and the paternal order that of day and light – whose God is Apollo, in the guise of Phoebus. The conflict between the two *dikai* is that between the Erinyes and Apollo, between an archaic and a new order of gods and of the polis: it is configured as a conflict between day and night, light and darkness. Their ambivalence marks the imagery of the play from the beginning. The "proof and token" of the fire beacon (*Agamemnon*, v. 315) is at the least ambiguous. For the watchman it means victory in Troy and the return of Agamemnon; for Clytemnestra, on the other hand, it means that she must make preparations for his murder. The stalemate of votes at the end of the negotiations makes it clear that the two positions are equal in value, although not in kind. Athena, as the representative of the new hierarchy of Gods, makes the decision: law is finally a question of power.

The two opposing claims, to the extent that they are mutually exclusive, are both at once lawful and unlawful (as Orestes suggests in Euripides, v. 647). Their conflict also grounds later re-workings of the myth in antiquity: the Electra dramas of Sophocles and Euripides, as well as the latter's *Orestes*. The aporetic nature of the conflict is indicated in two passages in Aeschylus. In the *Libation-Bearers* (v. 269ff), Orestes invokes the threat of Apollo: if he does not revenge his father, the wrath of the Erinyes will punish him with plague and madness. In the *Eumenides,* Athena likewise invokes the Erinyes, who will unleash a plague in response to an acquittal for Orestes – now not the avenger of his father, but the murderer of his mother. The disease is "a kind of figure for the justice that has not been done". And to the extent that the conflict of the *Oresteia* is between two positions of equal value and with equal justification, the *polis* remains marked in its deep structure by illness, even if the tribunal and the law as an orderly procedure instated with the conclusion of the trial seem to resolve the two positions. In the symptoms of plague in Blanchot's *Most High* – decomposing bodies, flames in the darkness, anguish at night, madness – the elements of the threat of Apollo and the Erinyes are still recognizable.

Martin Hose argues that with the acquittal at the end of the Eumenides, Orestes' "moral conflict is resolved", and that any interpretation that would see this decision as merely formal, and the "moral conflict as unresolved" would be "in error". This is more or less what Max Aue says too. When an orderly legal process, instituted by a stable order, acquits a murderer, even if he has in fact murdered his mother, then he is innocent, and his "moral conflict is resolved". An act that is correct within the framework of a prevailing legal system cannot be "morally" culpable. Christian Meier likewise suggests such a reading, while at the same time, making its fragility clear. The "decision by due process" is the solution, but of an insoluble conflict, and therefore no solution. As Karl Reinhardt wrote laconically: "The problem of the Oresteia has by no means disappeared. Not even juristically, let alone morally." Orestes remains, after all, the murderer of his mother. "No court of law can solve the moral problem in the case of Orestes, and this is not only the case in ancient Athens, but still today." Christian Meier takes over the essential core of Reinhardt's analysis. He shows how "each thesis is always supplemented by its antithesis" in the dramaturgical construction of the *Oresteia*, so that "victory and ill fate, fortune and guilt, are merely two sides of the same coin". "Everything has two sides to it."

Ambivalence is a pervasive medium of the dramatization; it characterizes above all the meaning of the whole complex; the question remains open if the curse which has created the nexus of guilt within the family history has been lifted, if real guilt can be overcome by a formal decision. The decision also has important consequences from a political point of view; it confirms the view that men have "the whole say and women none".[15] The play does not endorse this notion, but it does not simply criticize it either. It represents the process of decision in its integral undecidability, and shows how the decision is ratified by the female sacrifice at the origin of the new order. The Erinyes let themselves be persuaded by Athena, with the help of Peitho, to give up their demands (*Eumenides*, v. 885, 971). They are demoted to the status of extras in the new order, frightening but in fact powerless. But since their legitimate claim has not lapsed, anxiety remains a central component of the affective economy of the new political order: "the hounds of wrath that avenge a mother" (*Libation-Bearers*, v. 924) enter into the political unconscious, and return as symptoms of illness in the polis. Nomological knowledge is grounded in a nosological knowledge. The *Oresteia* is a spiritual site of memory, in that it dramatically articulates this elemental conflict. Orestes is the figure of this site: he is acquitted in order to bring an end to the cycle of blood vengeance demanded by talion law, but this acquittal conflicts with the idea of homicide entailing a guilt that has to be expiated.

Jean-Paul Sartre took up the conflict of the *Oresteia* in his play, *The Flies,* again staging it as a conflict of two opposing claims of right: the right of Aegisthus and that of Orestes – but also the right of the individual and that of the collective.[16] The people of

[15] Martin Hose: *Die Orestie des Aischylos – die Götter, das Recht und die Stadt*, in: Elke Stein-Hölkeskamp / Karl-Joachim Hölkeskamp (Hg.): *Die griechische Welt. Erinnerungsorte der Antike*, München, Beck, 2010, p. 432, 650; Christian Meier, *The Political Art of Greek Tragedy*, translated by Andrew Webber, Baltimore, Johns Hopkins U P, 1993, p. 113, 128, 134; Karl Reinhardt: *Aischylos als Regisseur und Theologe*, Bern, Francke, 1949, p. 79, 160.

[16] Jean-Paul Sartre: *Les mouches*, in: Jean Paul Sartre: *Théâtre complet*, edited by Michel Contat et al. Paris, Gallimard, 2005, p. 1–87 / *The Flies and In Camera*. Trans. Stuart Gilbert. London, Hamish Hamilton, 1946. This drama is cited in parentheses with act, scene and page-number; the first number is referring to the English translation, and the second to the original French.

the city of Argos are vitally concerned by the conflict in the house of the Atreides, and they are implicated in the guilt in Agamemnon's death. Jupiter refers to this situation from the very beginning. Why did the people of Argos not say anything or resist, when the lawful ruler of the city was murdered and an unjust rule was introduced? The guilt of the entire city is the *faute originelle* – "the original sin" (I, 1, p.14, 8), that is at the origin of the remorse defining the moral order of the city. This "inexpiable crime" of spouse-murder and regicide is common knowledge and borne by the whole community: it is an "official crime", nothing less than a "founding crime" (I, 5 p.32, 20). Orestes alone confronts this state of things. He is an outsider, and thus does not belong to the order of the city, but as a member of the Atreides family – and in fact their lawful ruler, after the death of Agamemnon – he wants above all to belong to it. He wants citizenship in Argos at any cost – "even by a crime" (I, 2, p. 14, 22). Thus, he wants to mediate his own fate with the general fate of the city. This clause "even by a crime" states the basic problem of the play; to save the law of the city by a crime, which by definition excludes one from citizenship. If the "moral order" of the city is itself criminal, founded on an official crime, then the law of the city is fundamentally unlawful. Orestes wants to break the unlawful law, and found a new law. What does it mean in such a constellation to say: "even by a crime"? Is a crime against an unlawful order even a crime or is it just? Logically, the negation of the negation would lead to its dialectical overcoming in a new law. But is the legal order logical? What is the law of the "moral order"? And what is resistance, what is freedom, in such a context? Such problems are implicit in the play, although not fully unfolded in the rather one-dimensional dramaturgy. At any rate, it should be clear at the end, when the Erinyes pounce on Orestes, how high Sartre sets the price of freedom.

Electra formulates the problem in all clarity: "An evil thing is only conquered by an evil thing" (II, 4, p. 52, 35). Therefore, while Orestes can proclaim the freedom of his action, and reject the attribution of guilt and remorse, he cannot avoid punishment; he is not thereby freed of the Erinyes. "I am not guilty" (III, 2, p. 88, 60) he tells Jupiter, marking the difference between his actions and those of Aegisthus, who does not fully recognize his own act, and thus falls prey to remorse. But they are both guilty, since they are murderers, as Electra suggests. "Something has happened and we are no longer free to blot it out" (II, 2, p. 79, 53). To be "not-guilty" is not a question of subjective decision; guilt does not disappear if one does not accept it; it is objective, grounded in the realities. Orestes is a murderer, and therefore the Erinyes pursue him. It is here that the innermost core of the problem of freedom is located. Freedom does not recognize the law, transgresses it, and pleads "not guilty" for its act. But it can in no way get around the law; even in transgressing the law, it remains subject to it. What is innocence from the perspective of freedom remains guilt from the perspective of the law, and demands punishment. Blanchot identified this predicament in the opposition of reality and meaning in the "Orestes myth"; freedom does not acknowledge the meaning of guilt, and refuses to acknowledge the right of the law to condemn its act, but it can still not eliminate its reality. The task and the effect of freedom is "to substitute for the Erinyes, goddesses at first of vengeance, then of remorse, the Erinyes who reign only in an empty sky".[17] (*Faux Pas*, 63, 76). They continue to impose their order, even if one no longer

[17] Maurice Blanchot: *Le mythe d'Oreste*, in: Maurice Blanchot: *Faux pas*, Paris, Gallimard, 1971.

believes in them, as Orestes warns his tutor, who dismisses them as a "superstition". "They will tear you into pieces alive" (III, 5, p. 96, 68).

In the free act, guilt and innocence correspond to each other; guilt is the shadow of the free act and punishment is its price. The aporetic nature of the conflict becomes apparent in the debate between Orestes and Jupiter. Jupiter accusingly produces a cosmological proof of guilt. The free acts of humans upset a world-order that is good, taken as a whole; the free man falls outside the world-order. The world is providentially created, and good; by his act, Orestes has introduced evil in the form of disorder, and is therefore himself evil. In his defense, Orestes invokes an anthropological proof of freedom. Jupiter is the ruler of the world, but not of humans, since he made them free. Freedom has now turned against him, and had to turn against him, since it is only in this way that it manifests itself as freedom (III, 2). Jupiter positions himself as the representative of good and of order, against Orestes, as the representative of disorder and evil. Orestes sees this order as oppression, and hence as evil; his own act is free and therefore good. What is good to the one is evil to the other, and each of the two arguments has its own internal rationality, given their own starting points. The arguments are equal in value, although not in kind. The basic conflict is analogous to that of the two *dikai* in Aeschylus.

In his commentary, Blanchot emphasizes this "insoluble situation in which whatever [Orestes] does, whether he abstains or whether he kills, he makes himself guilty". The *Oresteia* concerns the choice of Orestes to take the conflict upon himself, changing himself into this "night of evil and horror" in order "to enter into his fate". For this reason, the play is not so much the "personal drama of a hero"; Orestes is the site at which the suprapersonal conflict between the two orders and powers is worked out. For this reason, Blanchot's analysis of the problematic of the crime begins with the concept of innocence. Orestes comes to Argos as an innocent. "He is innocence but with the passive and inconstant innocence of someone who does not exist." His deed is the crime of crimes, a "crime pushed to the end [that] gives man a foretaste of a new innocence". This is the new innocence of freedom which, in accordance with the extremity of the crime, also takes over full responsibility for its ultimate consequences. "By crime he gives himself the possibility of being truly innocent." The result is "innocence inside evil": such innocence can indeed take away the meaning of guilt from evil, but in no way deny its reality.

In this intensification of the aporetic conflict of freedom as innocence inside evil, what is decisive is that it is not a matter of a moral or a legal exculpation, but a structural description. Innocence is the consequence of the co-existence of two forces that are equal in value, though not in kind. Freedom consists in deciding for one of the two sides; the evil lies in the consequence that every decision is guilty, so that innocence in evil is always also innocence in guilt. This situation determines the point of departure for Blanchot's re-working of the Orestes myth. Sartre conceives the conflict between freedom and law univocally in terms of the link between act and remorse. Blanchot reveals the implicit aporias. What is law, in view of the co-existence of the two *dikai*? And what is the status of freedom in view of the impossibility of transgressing the law?

([1]1943), p. 72-76 / Maurice Blanchot: *The myth of Orestes*, in: Maurice Blanchot: *Faux Pas*, translated by Charlotte Mandell. Stanford UP, 2002, p. 59-63.

What remains of the message of Orestes, who engages himself for freedom, when the engagement finds itself entangled in these aporias? What does it mean when Blanchot sees the freedom of Orestes in his will "to enter into his own fate"? And what becomes of the myth of Orestes itself, when it is confronted with such a structure?

The difference between *The Most High* and Camus' *The Plague* is to be understood within the same field. When Camus won the *Prix des Critiques* in summer of 1947, Blanchot told a journalist from *Combat* who asked him why he had abstained from the vote that he had not read the novel. What may have sounded a little strange at the time made more sense a year later, with the publication of *The Most High*. The superficial similarity is obvious – each novel takes an epidemic as an allegory for the dysfunctional social and political relations of a state. The difference is located at the level of the content. Camus constructs his novel within the horizon of a theodicy; it bears on the metaphysical question of God and his justification in face of the evil and suffering in the world; these problems are explored in the debates between the atheist Dr Rieux and the Catholic priest, Paneloux. Blanchot's novel unfolds in the horizon of history; it bears on the political question of the law and its justice in face of internal conflict and revolt within society; these questions are developed in the debates between the rebel Bouxx, who is also a doctor, and the "good citizen", Henri Sorge (16, 24). As the distinction between the godless and the lawless suggests, the question of theodicy here becomes a political question. "World-history is the world's court": thus Schiller, in his poem *Resignation* (1786), drew the conclusions from the theodicy debate after the earthquake of Lisbon, as Rousseau had earlier in his debate with Voltaire. And Hegel subsequently elaborated the idea in philosophical-historical terms.

Blanchot poses this question in a radically new mode after the civilizational break marked by the Shoa. It is not only the theological justification, but also the political justification of law, society and state which has been shattered. Hegel still wanted to justify the state in the name of the unfolding of reason, of which it was the last and historically real form. The madness of the present – *La folie du jour*, or *The Madness of the Day* is the title of Blanchot's *récit* on the relationship of madness and law – has dissolved the law in both of its forms, both canonical and civil. Civilization, represented by Henri Sorge, slips into psychosis. The true God of Christianity and the real God of the state have turned into the delusional God of madness, the God as which and through which the psychotic tries to reconfigure the broken world. Like Daniel Paul Schreber in the *Memoirs of my Nervous Illness* (1903), Henri Sorge exhibits the wild, uncontained configuration that is designated in psychopathological terms as psychosis. With the figure of Sorge, the novel explores what will become of the world after the end of the law. The catastrophe of the madness of the present is a theological-political catastrophe, and as such, a symbolic catastrophe: the collapse of the world as a totality of meaning. The name of Sorge is no doubt also to be understood as an echo of *Sorge* (Care), the term which Heidegger uses to name the configuring agent on the world-relations in *Being and Time*.

Faced with the delusional God of psychosis, questions of justification become absurd: when the symbolic order is broken, such questions are nonsensical; their meaning is unintelligible. Nonetheless, out of the depths of misery, the world calls for justice. At the end of the novel, Sorge's companion cites the Psalm, *De Profundis*, meant to be sung on the way to Jerusalem; it poses the question: "I know that you are the Unique, the Supreme One. Who could stay standing before you?" (MH, 233, 224). This lends a different aspect to the problem of theodicy. What becomes of justice and justification when neither salvational history nor world-history represents the "world-court", when the misery of the present is not justified by any higher order of reasons in the future? Psychosis is the mental disposition corresponding to what Camus names as the absurd. After the collapse of the signifying articulations within the symbolic order, the absurdity of the senseless is the essence of the modern experience. Blanchot unfolds this absurdity in terms of the impossibility of distinguishing law and lawlessness. Littell makes it into the epic of the real and existing anomie of National Socialism.

Henri Sorge is "anybody" (MH, 1, 9; 22, 28; 233, 223), an Everyman-figure, who poses the question of the humanity of the human. The question is explored through Sorge's relations with others, and in his relation to "the Law", the public order. As an employee in the city administration, Sorge is a part of the public order, and an agent of "the Law". Since the family forms the point of articulation between the individual and collective, the question of what it means "to have a family" is central to the novel (MH, 2, 10). The family has an archaic deep structure: this is its mythic dimension. "I realized that all of this could have taken place at some other time, thousands of years ago, as if time had opened and I had fallen through the crack [...] This went a long way back. My mother now was someone from before, a monumental person who could lead me into totally crazy things. That's what the family was. The recollection of the period before the law [...]" (MH, 3, 11). His sister, too, has something "backward" about her, that makes her "seem of another time" (MH, 15, 22). The family imposes the dominance of the past; in his meeting with his sister, with her "very old eyes", Sorge "trembled not only in the present, but also in the past, and perhaps only in the past" (MH, 51, 55). The past is effective and real in an absolute way; such is the power of the old stories, which prescribe modes of understanding and modes of behaviour, and configure the life of the individuals and the community that they form.

Public life is represented in various aspects of socialization; people in the neighbourhood, on the street, in the restaurants, in the cinema, at sporting events, in mass-gatherings, at work. The "law" is the ordering agent of public life, mediating the disparate individuals with the state. "That everyone was equally faithful to the law – ah, that idea intoxicated me" (MH, 18, 26). Everyone acts "in their own interests [...] and yet there was a halo of light around these hidden lives. [...] So I asked myself, what is this State? It's in me, I feel its existence in everything I do, through every fibre in my body." Hence "a report on the day [...] a report, by that I mean a simple diary", the report of a man who, like Henri Sorge, is simply "anyone", would be "a supreme truth, the same one that circulated actively between all of us, a truth that public life constantly relaunched" (MH, 18-19, 26). Through the pre-established harmony of the law – such being the Hegelian basic assumption – the individual is at all moments the perfect representative of the universal embodied in the state. He guarantees the continuity of order, law and history. A breakdown of the individual then implies that "history would collapse" (MH, 24, 30). The family is the extra-legal agent of this breakdown. The truth and order of the law disintegrate to the extent that the individual belongs to another order – "before the law" – by his relation to his family. The law makes an absolute claim to regulate the life of the individual. And yet essential elements of the constitution of this individual, deriving from the family, as the other form of his identity, stand outside the law. The result is an elementary schizoid trait: para-nomia and paranoia as the disposition of the individual.

For this reason, if *The Most High* is a novel of the law, then, it must also be a novel of freedom. Sorge's words – I will regain my freedom – *Je reprends ma liberté* – function as the articulating center of the novel: not only its arithmetical center (or close to it), but above all, its conceptual center (MH, 127, 124). The question of freedom divides the novel into two halves. In the first part, Sorge, the "submissive Orestes" (Foucault), remains passive, refusing to challenge his stepfather, the representative of the all-powerful law, and declaring any kind of resistance to be meaningless and futile; in the second part, he becomes an activist and seeks to make contact with the resistance-group led by Bouxx. In the process, he identifies increasingly with the Law and finally, in a psychotic hyperbole, becomes himself the *Most High*, the State itself, the "real God", as Hegel conceived it.

In the first half of the novel, the question of freedom is developed under various aspects in a number of episodes and stories involving resistance against the law. Sorge's basic attitude consists in identifying with his citizenship. He needs to "be a good citizen" (MH, 16, 24; 130, 128), and feels that the state lives within him: "It's in me, I feel its existence in everything I do, through every fibre of my body" (MH, 19, 26). But he is confronted with moments that challenge this stance, and threaten to destroy it. In the Metro, a man has stolen a woman's wallet. Sorge finds this "just unbelievable". How is it possible that someone can steal, and place himself outside of the law? The solution is remarkable. The man has certainly stolen, but all the same, he is not outside the law. It is not a transgression: "it was just a sham, a kind of game to make the law circulate, to recall to everyone the depth and intangibility of liberty." The theft sets the law in motion; not only does the thief not stand outside the law; the law and the state need him in order to state and to communicate: "We possess truth, peace and law, and this person steals, not because he's outside of justice, but because the state needs this example, and from time to time it's necessary to create an interruption through which history and the past can rush" (MH, 28, 34). The transgression of the law leads to its fulfilment: in this figure of thought, by which the negation of something leads to something new on a higher level, one can see the formal structure of the Hegelian dialectic; the negation is productive; the negation is put into the service of history. Nothing escapes this movement of co-optation, transforming every negation into something positive. Any kind of transgression is brought back into the space of the law, which now becomes absolute and total; there is no outside, and cannot possibly be.

When the law is total and totalitarian to this extent, resistance becomes absurd and impossible. Any attempt to break out of the space of the law only strengthens its power and expands its domain. The logic is developed still further in another story concerning a thief. A cashier who is guilty of irregularities (as the expression has it) is accused not of theft, but of sabotage. Sorge explains this on the premise that "nothing stands above the law"; thus all crimes against the law are conspiracy and sabotage (MH, 41, 46). Since a transgression of the law is not possible, any kind of offence puts in question the legitimacy of the law. Theft is therefore the most horrific crime imaginable, a revolt against the legality of the law. But it is a crime which cannot be committed; it fails since the law brings everything into communication with itself. Therefore all that remains visible of the terrible crime of revolt is only "an insignificant trace, the theft"

(MH, 41, 47). And for this theft, too, the same explanation applies as in the first story of theft.

Such sophisms are one of the main characteristics of the novel. They point to a problem that is inscribed in the law and the political order that it governs, and that manifests itself fully in Henri Sorge. In Sorge's psychosis, the basic fragility of the law is revealed. In Rousseau's treatise *The Social Contract*, we find similar considerations. It follows from the consent given to the general will that the death penalty can be necessary for someone who harms the general will: "Moreover, every wrongdoer, in attacking the rights of society by his crimes, becomes a rebel and a traitor to his country. By violating its laws he ceases to belong to it, and is even making war on it [....]. When a criminal is put to death, it is as an enemy rather than as a citizen." Hegel in the *Elements of a Philosophy of Right* determines crime as "an injury [...] to the universal cause [*Sache*]", and this "gives rise to the viewpoint that an action may be a *danger* to society".[18]

Against the rebel Bouxx, Sorge exclaims: "you aren't teaching me anything, you're only expressing what I think, and when you speak, it's me who's speaking" (MH, 42, 47). Here he wants to underline his ideas on the omnipotence of the law, and to make Bouxx understand the futility of his resistance activity. What happens, however, is that rather than Sorge drawing nearer to the resistance, the resistance approaches the law. Sorge sees the danger of such a convergence. His recognition: "You're like me – *vous êtes mon semblable*" (MH, 44, 49) – is spoken from the perspective of the law: but it allows at any moment the reversal: "I am your equal and similar to you."

The advancing dissociation of personality and world-perception is marked by the impossibility of maintaining the border between Sorge's perceptions and the reality of the world in which he lives. This impossibility applies both for Sorge and for the reader. Since Sorge narrates his story in the first person, there is no objective narrative instance that would denote a definite point of reference. The nurse in the clinic is identified with Sorge's sister, the clinic with his apartment, and the carer or doctor with Bouxx (MH, 77-80). It may be that the whole complex of the resistance exists only in Sorge's imagination, an ideation that has become a real phantasm, an apparition in the real, in the form of the doctor in the clinic. Sorge knows: "It makes no difference whether I'm sick or not" (MH, 79, 80).

Bouxx, on the other hand, insists on his political activities. On this level, Bouxx and Sorge are complementary figures of law and resistance. Bouxx declares his sympathy with the oppressed, and is an avowed insurgent, even seeking to win over Sorge for the revolutionary cause. Sorge counters with the lesson of the stories of the thieves. The struggle against the law only strengthens its power: "the government knows everything, and everything that happens does so with its complicity, and at its instigation" (MH, 43,

[18] Jean-Jacques Rousseau: *Du contrat social*, in: Jean-Jacques Rousseau: *Œuvres complètes*, III: *Du contrat social. Ecrits politiques*, edited by Bernard Gagnebin and Marcel Raymond, Paris, Gallimard, 1964 / *Discourse on Political Economy and The Social Contract*, translated by Christopher Betts. Oxford World Classics, 1994, II, 5, p. 376, 71-72.
Georg Wilhelm Friedrich Hegel: *Grundlinien der Philosophie des Rechts oder Naturrecht und Staatswissenschaft im Grundrisse* in: Georg Wilhelm Friedrich Hegel: *Werke*, Bd. 7, edited by Eva Moldenhauer and Karl Markus Michel, Frankfurt a. M., Suhrkamp, 1975 / *Elements in the Philosophy of Right*, translated by H.B. Nisbet, Cambridge, UP, 1991, § 218.

48). The talk of injustice and oppression is just the prattle of pamphlets: "The truth is that all these criticisms are prompted by the law itself: it needs them, and it is grateful to you for them" (MH, 48, 53). If the reality of the law is totalitarian, however, there remains the question of the *hors-la-loi*, of the necessity of an outside to the all-embracing interior of the law. Since the law homogenizes everything, making everything that is unequal, foreign and heterogeneous into the identical and the known, the question of the status and the location of the other inevitably arise. This other appears in the form of the insurgents in the novel, the *hors la loi*. The schizoid state of Sorge corresponds to the ongoing class-struggle, which is in the process of transforming into civil war.

The locus of the other is also occupied by the women in Sorge's life. Parallel to this discussion of revolutionary activity and to his relationship to Bouxx, Sorge tells of his relationship to Marie Scadran. He describes his meeting with her as the dissolution of all commonality. All that he has in common with her disappears during their meeting, and she becomes "something other"."For a few moments, you touch something foreign – believe me, you really feel it. It's not just a sensation, it's indisputable, it's horribly clear" (MH, 47, 52). In the report about the encounter itself, the point is made even more starkly. At first, Sorge sees only what they have in common. If every individual incarnates the law, each encounter becomes a union with him in the law. Before the law, and as human beings, they form a "community"; in touching the woman, he would "touch the law" (MH, 34-35). The couple is the minimal form of socialization, outside of the family, and thus an elementary figure of the law. "The reconciling Yes, in which the two I's let go their antithetical existence, is the existence of the I which has expanded into a duality [...] It is God manifested in the midst of those who know themselves in the form of pure knowledge." This passage in the *Phenomenology of Spirit* corresponds to the transition from morality to ethical life in the *Elements of the Philosophy of Right*. Ethical life as the kingdom of the law is the "manifest God", the mediator which makes the state into the "real God".[19]

Sorge experiences this common element dissolving in the encounter; it appears something alien. "It was then that she was transformed – I swear, she became different. And I myself became someone else." The encounter is not unification, becoming-one, but separation and estrangement. What until now had been a "truly common body" before the universal law, bringing everything on to the same level, breaks apart, and becomes recognizable in the encounter in its irreducible particularity. "Yes, I swear it: I had become a stranger, and the more I held her the more I felt her become a stranger, determined to show me someone and something different [...] at that moment, we became separated, we felt and breathed the separation, we gave it a body" (MH, 39, 44).

[19] Georg Wilhelm Friedrich Hegel: *Phänomenologie des Geistes* in: Georg Wilhelm Friedrich Hegel: *Werke*, Bd. 3, edited by Eva Moldenhauer und Karl Markus. Michel, Frankfurt a. M., Suhrkamp, 1976 / *Phenomenology of Spirit*, translated by A.V. Miller, Oxford, UP, 1976, p. 494, 407.
Georg Wilhelm Friedrich Hegel: *Grundlinien der Philosophie des Rechts oder Naturrecht und Staatswissenschaft im Grundrisse* in: Georg Wilhelm Friedrich Hegel: *Werke*, Bd. 7, edited by Eva Moldenhauer and Karl Markus Michel, Frankfurt a. M., Suhrkamp, 1975 / *Elements in the Philosophy of Right*, translated by H.B. Nisbet, Cambridge, UP, 1991, § 140, 218.

Sorge here brings out an essential moment of the encounter with the other; it is the articulation with a particular otherness, which, by its particularity, excludes a common space. The "truly common body" reduces this moment of particularity and otherness, and ensures that no encounter can really take place. Sorge resolves the aporia of alterity by experiencing the encounter as separation; the pair does not form a common body, they do not become "one flesh", as in the traditional conception; rather, they give a body to separation, making dissociation into the reality of the encounter.[20]

The disintegration of the "community" of the "truly common body" comes about when a foreign element is introduced by the superimposition of Marie Scadran (and later of the nurse, Jeanne Galgat) upon the figure of Sorge's sister Louise. Since the family is a "recollection of the period before the law" (MH, 3, 11), it becomes a disturbing factor in the "community" of the law. It forms the uncanny ground of the individual personality, the abyss of the law. As such, it corresponds structurally to the rebel underground. Sorge's sister, Louise, – and mediated through her, his mother – is the agent of his attachment to the past. This attachment is configured in an uncontained hatred of the mother, and an equally uncontained love for the father. This basic conflict of ambivalence between love and hate can be designated as the Oresteian complex. Louise preserves the power of the past by her cult-like veneration for the memory of their dead father. Her room is a "sanctuary" (MH, 58, 62). The image that she keeps of him is a "true icon" (MH, 52, 56). As she shows it to Sorge, the two faces are superimposed; she holds up the frame from behind, so that Sorge sees her face at the same time, along with the portrait (MH, 52, 56). This scene corresponds to that in the cemetery, at the family memorial, when Louise places herself in a "kind of niche", and Sorge sees her looking at him "in such a strange frozen way that I didn't feel that it was her eyes but rather that behind them there was something – and perhaps nothing – doing the looking" (MH, 71, 74).

The relation of image to the past is that which exists "before the law". This becomes very clear with the passage on the threadbare and moth-eaten tapestry in Louise's room. The tapestry is very old, and it is an image of "something very old, criminally old": it is "a false and perfidious image, vanished and indestructible" (MH, 58, 54). A horse, rearing up "in rage, suffering and hatred" gives a vaguely concrete, but at the same time completely unclear form to the image. The horse derives from an iconic tradition – following the myth of the horses of the soul in Plato's *Phaedrus* – which gives the soul a physical form. This image looks [*elle m'épiait*] at Sorge, as he looks at it [*je l'épiais*]. The little moths which fly up out of it are the figures of this dissociative image-reality at the limit of the formless. They are "the agents of a horrible and dead past", and they seek to lure Sorge "into the deadest and most horrible past" (MH, 54, 58). The family is evidently the relation of image to the past, the relation to the past that is contained in the

[20] In Blanchot's later literary texts, the encounter of man and woman as an allegory of the encounter with the other and the alien is an essential theme. *The Most High* explores the conditions of possibility of such an encounter with the other in its relation to the law, as the agent of the community. If the law forms a "truly common body", which breaks into two in the encounter, then such an alienation is a possible form of the outside of the law. At this time, Blanchot's friend, Georges Bataille, was also seeking to think the violation of the law in terms of eroticism, which he understands as an elemental transgression.

image. The scene in the family tomb reduces this situation back to a void. It is "an empty room, just a simple tomb, clean and cold – and empty" (MH, 71, 74). The empty room becomes a void, which then becomes Sorge himself; he stops breathing and then, he says, "the void itself made me breathe":"the void filled me with a substance that was heavier, fuller, more crushing than me" (MH, 71, 74). No doubt it is the substance of the dead father that is present here as a void.

The stepfather, like the father, forms the side of the family that is turned towards the law. Both belong to the leading circles of the city. On the national day of mourning, Sorge's dead father is publicly mourned, and a giant catafalque is carried through the city in a parade.[21] The parade unites the citizens of the city in "national mourning" (MH, 75, 76-77). The visit to the family tomb corresponds to the public parade with "a gigantic catafalque"; the constitution of the family corresponds to that of the public sphere; the state of Sorge's personality, which comes from the family, reflects the state of the law, which is clearly based in the same family structure.[22]

The stepfather suggests that the epidemic in the city could be a propagandistic invention of the government, and even that the fires lit by the revolutionaries could be "sabotage" and serve the interest of the government: "what burns will be exactly what must burn" (MH, 64, 67). Sorge's illness takes the form of a burning fever (MH, 79, 80); this is part of the network of correspondences linking his condition with the public events. Sorge's stepfather remarks that the fires are "something very old and collective":"When you see a house burn, you always get the impression it's something from long ago, that an old feeling, an old bitterness started the fire" (MH, 63, 67). They are signs of the archaic in the political – of the conflict-structure of the political and of the law itself. The actions of the rebels and the class-struggle in the public space correspond to the conflict-structure of the family. For this reason, Bouxx represents the other side of Sorge's personality.

The old histories "come from the dawn of time": the details change but it is "always the same event" (MH, 87, 88). The repetition compulsion arises because these histories have "not completely" taken place, and exist only as "incomprehensible and absurd outlines", which are about to be realized in the present. "Now's the time, everything's reappearing, everything's being revealed clearly and truthfully", Sorge claims, citing the *Dies Irae*. He perceives "other more distant faces" standing behind the family members. The old histories will reach completion in himself. "Now is when we're going to understand the truth about all the horrible things [...] It's going to be settled and judged once and for all, according to the law" (MH, 89, 88-89). The state of Sorge's personality is the truth of the history that culminates in him. This is his anti-Hegelian project; it reveals what remains un-thought in Hegel's philosophy of history. But it is also Sorge's psychosis – and it remains true, as he says, that "it makes no difference whether I'm sick or not" (MH, 79, 80).The truth of history is the manifestation of psychosis, psychosis as apocalypse, "an insane sun" (MH, 106. 105). Psychosis reveals the truth of the state and the law. The dissociation of Sorge's personality corresponds stage by stage to

21 In Sartre's *The Flies*, Kreon, too, has the dead Agamemnon publicly and ceremonially mourned.

22 Littell takes up this idea with the correspondence perceived by Max Aue between his father and Hitler.

the dissolution of the order of the state and to his shift closer to the resistance. It remains an open question whether the possibility of rebellion makes him ill, or whether the illness is the breakdown of personality configured by the law, and sets free the possibility of the rebellion in him. The paranomic dimension of resistance and rebellion is also psychosis. And its constitution is furnished by the Orestes myth.

In Sartre's *The Flies*, the meaning of the Oresteian predicament is freedom. Aeschylus' Orestes also stands outside the law, as one sees from the tie in the votes when his act is judged at the end of the *Eumenides*. The law cannot make the decision purely in its own terms. The sovereign instance of Athena, the deciding god, is needed. Hence Sorge, too, has to become "God". His apotheosis is the consequence of his freedom, and at the same time the peak of his psychosis. Freedom from the law turns into madness.

The antinomic structure of the law is set out in the discussion between Sorge and his stepfather on law and freedom. Its central figure is the epidemic. Since antiquity, the plague as an illness of the body politic has functioned as a figure for the disturbance of political order. That which is epidemic is propagated throughout the *demos*. This applies first and foremost to the law; it is essentially epidemic. In *Peri Archon – De principiis*, the Church father Origenes uses the word epidemic synonymously with *parousia*. The presence of Christ in the world is epidemic because it re-configures the *demos*.[23]

The epidemic in the novel is also a figure of resistance to the law. It is at once both law and resistance. The characters Bouxx and Sorge's stepfather are the figures of this antinomy, and represent two sides of Sorge's personality. Sorge recognizes that his stepfather is taking his place: "he was my living, working part; he was my health" (MH, 121, 119). Bouxx, on the other hand, takes the place of Sorge's stepfather, and Sorge admits that he is "having a hard time separating the two" (MH, 137, 134).

The law rules the city through a surveillance apparatus, mockingly referred to as the "fly-department" (MH, 66, 69).[24] The regime knows everything about the citizens; thus Sorge's stepfather knows about his relationship with Marie Scadran. The transparency of the citizen follows from the "epidemic" character of the law, which completely mediates every individual with the collectice. The private domain is therefore always public before the law. As the official is entirely identified with his function (MH, 129, 126), the individual is only a citizen, and the desire for privacy is extinguished: "the most intimate decisions are immediately integrated into the forms of public usefulness, from which they are inseparable" (MH, 136, 133). When the particular will is completely

23 "We must say, also, that the divinity of the prophetic declarations and the spiritual nature of the law of Moses shone forth after the advent of Christ (*epidemésantos Iesou*)", in: Origen: *On the Principles*, translated by Frederick Crombie in: *Anti-Nicene Fathers* Vol 4, edited by Alexander Roberts et al., Buffalo, Christian Literature Publishing, 1885, IV i, 6: see also IV, i, 3; IV i, 5; IV ii, 1; IV ii, 6.

24 In the early 18th century, police informers were referred to by the police themselves euphemistically as *personnes de confiance*, and in the jargon of the people as *mouches*, flies. See: Gerhard Sälter: *Gerüchte als subversives Medium. Das Gespenst der öffentlichen Meinung und die Pariser Polizei zu Beginn des 18. Jahrhunderts*, in: *Werkstatt Geschichte* 15 (1996), p. 12. In his *Reveries*, Rousseau refers to a man whom he takes to be one of his persecutors as "une de ces mouches qu'on tient sans cesse à mes trousses". See: Jean-Jacques Rousseau: *Les rêveries du promeneur solitaire*, in: Jean-Jacques Rousseau: *Œuvres complètes* I, edited by Bernard Gagnebin und Marcel Raymond, Paris, Gallimard, 1959, p. 1090.

configured by the general will, surveillance is not experienced as a restriction, but as the fulfilment of the particular will. For the citizen, "the police are no more, they've disappeared, they're the overturned image one never sees, required by the uprightness of all things" (MH, 134, 131). Under these conditions, the state and history have come to their end – Sorge's stepfather takes up Alexander Kojève's interpretation of Hegel –; the "last word" of history has been spoken, its truth has been revealed, but this end is of "endless duration". Sorge views this ironically, saying that he sounds like "a law-professor speaking in class", and points out that there is still sickness and poverty, in other words, exceptions to the law (MH, 134-135, 132-133).

Bouxx therefore comes at once in place of the stepfather into Sorge's room, and talks of the resistance (MH, 137, 134). This is one of the moments in which it seems as if the whole history could be a projection of Sorge's madness. Sorge then "is" both the stepfather and the law, both Bouxx and the resistance. This would mean that the law has in fact integrated its own antithetical opposite into itself, in which case the stepfather's position would be correct. But it could also be that Sorge loses his sanity due to the irreconcilable tension between the law and the resistance; the tension of the continual state of exception engenders madness. The alternative remains undecidable, both for Sorge and the reader. If the law is the truth, then Bouxx's desire to fight it is merely pathological. If he is truly a "dissident", then the state is a "deception" and the resistance fights for justice. But even then the resistance is only an "instrument of the state", which is expelled in the name of the law, and in this way, wakes the law into life. Sorge incarnates this paranoid circle, in which even the resistance is an instrument of the law, the means by which it marks the location of the outside and is thus able to incorporate it.

The Most High becomes increasingly recognizable as a report written from within psychosis: "the events were recorded, were written, and they made a story by the simple fact that I was there" (MH, 147, 144). The events are the report that recounts them; in this report, madness makes the world into a proliferating network of relations, into which everything can be integrated. The location shifts from apartment block to clinic, to prison, to camp; one cannot decide between reality and imagination, between thought, fantasy and madness. The burning abscess in Sorge's leg, the fervency of his reflections, and the fire in the city are related and pass into each other (MH, 66, 69; 79, 80; 146, 149); for Sorge, the burning in his leg and the fires in the city are the same phenomenon. The throbbing of the wound mutates into the thumping by which he communicates with the inhabitant of the next room (MH, 145-147, 142-144). Words are transformed into what they refer to and things dissolve into their names, as the distinction between the two becomes fluid. The word "prison" "had a visible and brilliant form, as brilliant as the word 'fire' a little while ago" (MH, 155, 158). The nominalism of signs is the linguistic-philosophical dimension of the psychosis.

Words and things converge upon the image, and become indistinguishable within it. The symbolic order of the clear and distinct, of conceptually distinct abstract thought, collapses; thinking regresses from the symbolic to the imaginary. The linguistic-philosophical turn that Lacan introduces into psychoanalysis shows the father and the law as the ordering instance of the symbolic. The imaginary by contrast is the domain of the mother. Madness is the proliferation of images in a delusional pattern of correspondences. The Orestes myth works this conflict out in terms of the two *dikai*. On the

mythic level, the story of Orestes concerns the agon of the maternal and the paternal orders: on the psychological level, it concerns the conflict of the imaginary and the symbolic; on the linguistic level, the conflict of image and concept.
When the symbolic order disintegrates, the law becomes antinomic, as the development of the resistance shows. What Bouxx thinks he is opposing to the law only strengthens it. "The law is cunning." Like Hegel's reason, it is able to integrate the negative and the resistance that opposes it: this is why it is "absolute truth" (MH, 178, 173). From this, Bouxx draws the "rather strange conclusion" that he should make allies of the officials, the representatives of the law. But through the affirmation, which is the form the resistance takes, he becomes himself the representative of the law: he becomes something like "his own spy" (MH, 206, 197-198). After the upheavals caused by the epidemic, Bouxx in a certain manner assumes the rule; the "spirit of lawlessness" has taken the place of the law and a "false authority" dominates the state. The commands of Bouxx have legal force – *force de loi* (MH, 216, 208). The implication is that where the law reigns as an absolute power, capable of integrating its own opposite, the opposite can become the law, to the point that it is impossible to decide what is "justice" and what is "terrorism" (MH, 229, 219). The law is impersonated by a sequence of substitutes and usurpers. Bouxx takes the place of Sorge's stepfather, who himself took the place of Sorge's father. The myth of the Atreides shows violence and crime as the deep structure of law and power. The law and its usurpation by the resistance, the legal order and its disturbance by crime cannot be distinguished. "Where is the law? What does it do? These screams now were terrible" (MH, 228, 219). Sorge in his psychotic state as the Most High is the figure of the essential antinomy of the law, the moment of the indifference of opposites (MH, 230-233, 221-224).

Sorge asks himself at times, how it would be, if his "true father" ruled in the place of his step-father. This is the deciding question of the Oresteian complex, which Littell will explore further. The Oresteian condition is premised on the fact that the "the true father" is dead; the stepfather has taken his place and usurped the law. The question then is what "a true father" is, and what a stepfather or a false father is, and how they are to be distinguished. If the "Father" is the instance of the validity of the law, would a false father be the instance of a false symbolization of the law? But is the "true father" not a *petitio principii*? If the false father, the false authority, with its "spirit of unlawfulness", rules, then "the commands of the Führer have legal force" (K 101, 100-101; 566, 522). But this would also hold true for the "true father".

Another figure of indifference is the stain which Sorge perceives ever again; now as a black stain on the wall, now as a red stain on the fabric of his sister's dress. In the red stain, on which the dripping water forms a black stain, the two converge (MH, 235, 225). The stain is formless, a figure of the non-figural, of that which is no longer or not yet a figure. "I knew this stain well. I saw it for the first time at my parents', quietly resting on the wall behind the sofa. It sprawled on the clinic wall, across from me [...]. Here it was the result of water leakage. This stain was unusual in that it was only a stain. It represented nothing, had no color, and, except for dusty permeation, nothing made it visible. Was it even visible? It didn't exist under the wallpaper; it had no form, but resembled something dirty, spoiled, but clean as well" (MH, 43,

48).[25] The colour red links the various female figures: the black stain links Sorge's parents' house, his apartment, the clinic and the prison. The "accursed cunning of this whole business" (MH, 236, 226) – not the cunning of reason, but the cunning of madness – consists in the intertwining of these motifs – family, love and politics.

It is conceivable that Sorge's fantasies and delusions arise, like Rorschach associations, from this stain. At the beginning of the novel, Sorge thinks of writing a report on his day, and on his whole life, and comments: "I was certain then that all I had to do was write, hour by hour, a commentary on my activities, in order to find in them a blossoming of a supreme truth" (MH, 19, 26). The report, his writing, is the story, which takes phantasmatic reality for him: "what was happening right now, the room [...] I wrote it (and at the same time everything that was happening outside)" (MH, 107, 104).[26] The various dimensions of the story – Sorge, the family, the beloved, the public space, the state, the opposition, the *hors-la-loi* – are so many structural moments in the personality of Sorge, who is "anybody" (MH, 1, 9; 22, 28; 233, 223): an Everyman as the Most High. "So I asked myself, what is this State? It's in me, I feel its existence in everything I do, through every fiber of my body" (MH, 19, 26). As he writes his story down, he liberates this state of mind. The divinization of Everyman is the story of a madness, since this condition is profoundly antinomic.

To the extent that the law guarantees the order of the world, the antinomy of the law leads to total collapse, "to the point where everything that had been done was completely nullified, completely reduced to nothing". This is the apocalypse of psychosis, an apocalypse that takes place as the collapse of the order prevailing in the world. Therefore at the end, "everything was as before", but it no longer has the order of a world (MH, 247, 236). This conclusion is prefigured by the stain, in the various forms it has assumed. At the end it becomes the formless heap, which as at the same time, a hole: a morphological and topological monstrosity, the infinitude and limitlessness of the *apeiron* corresponding to the Most High, the unformed on the horizon of forms: "I saw something flow, solidify, flow again [...] these wrinkles, these excrescences, this surface of dry mud its crushed insides, this earthen heap its amorphous exterior, it didn't start anywhere, it didn't end anywhere, it didn't matter which side you caught it from, and once its form was half perceived it flattened out and fell back into a mass from which eyes could never get free" (MH, 248, 237). They eye which cannot free itself from what it sees, becomes literal eyes on the surface of the heap: "They weren't looking at me [...] I myself saw them no more than if they had been my own eyes, and already I was very close to them, dangerously close – who had ever been that close? [...] I saw and understood everything" (MH, 248-249). This is the figure of absolute knowledge, knowledge knowing itself – *noesis noesos* (Aristotle: *Metaphysics* XII, 9, 1074b34) – under the condition of psychosis. When Sorge at the end says "I speak", he announces the narrative of an experience that has already begun, that of *The Most High*.

Two remarks of Sorge to Bouxx, reproduced as the epigraph to the novel, propose this antinomic figure of thought in concentrated form. They show that Sorge makes this

[25] Cf. MH, 58, 61; 72, 75; 78, 77; 94-95, 94-95; 105, 105; 121, 119; 125, 128; 146, 143; 151, 147-148; 194-195, 188; 232, 223; 244, 234; 248, 237.

[26] "The events were recorded, they were written and made a story by the simple fact that I was there" (MH, 147). Cf. MH, 144, 141; 149, 146; 153, 149.

structure into the condition of his thought and personality. The antinomic constitution of the law – law and resistance conditioning and implying each other reciprocally – leads in the final instance to the undecidability of truth and lie, which are two moments of one process. As Sorge identifies with this figure of undecidability, his personality dissolves. His attitude can be epitomized in the Christomorphic formulation: I am the law, the truth and the resistance. The novel unfolds this state of mind in the figure of Henri Sorge, and shows it to be also the state of the law and of politics. It also reveals its historical dimension, in referring it back to "the old stories", and making their mythic deep structure visible. This is why Sorge is an Orestes: the story of Orestes is the mythic figuration of this condition.

In the novel, the two opposed orders that have shown themselves to be basic structuring elements of the Orestes myth, are the state-power, representing the law, and the organization of the resistance fighters, who fight the law. Those who fight for a new order are rebels, in that they oppose the old order. This conflict works itself out within the protagonist, Sorge. A "submissive Orestes", he identifies himself first with the law and the order of his stepfather; but since the stepfather has usurped the role of the father, he also identifies with the resistance. The latent internal conflict of the resulting psychic disposition leads to the dissociation of his personality, to psychosis, in which Sorge himself phantasmatically assumes the position of the law. Sorge's conflict is that he condemns and rejects what is nearest and dearest to him, the law, but does not want to acknowledge this: hence what he has rejected reappears in the form of a phantasm within the real order – the resistance of the lawless. This is why he is ill, and schizophrenic, in the literal sense of the word, divided. The division has its ground in the family romance and its structure. In *The Most High*, Blanchot lays bare the psychotic ground of the Atreides myth; the conflict of the two *dikai* is the schizoid ground of the psychotic and the political.

Sorge seeks to escape the "old histories" and their repetition compulsion; this is why he is at first a "submissive Orestes", who refuses the duty of revenge, the fight against the usurper, his stepfather. The novel leaves open the possibility that the history of Henri Sorge could be entirely the syndrome of a psychotic mind, for which the figuration of law and resistance, that is, the entire machinery of the state, becomes a phantasm. The psychotic system-production, for which the "apparatus of influence" (Victor Tausk) becomes a state-apparatus, is possible and necessary because there is a corresponding "real" mechanism which triggers the conflict: namely, the family romance, which is the cause of the illness and which generates the psychotic delusion. Conversely, the "real" structure of the political, the real political apparatus appears as the realization of the psychotic phantasm, whose deep structure is that of the family relations of the Atreides. Thus the Oresteian complex is the psychic dispositive of the political.

3 Nomos

Hard is the struggle to decide.
Aeschylus, *Agamemnon*, v. 1560.

The antinomic constitution of the law can be elaborated more rigorously by way of a reflection on modern political theory. In the 17th century, Thomas Hobbes wrote *Leviathan* as a theory of the *commonwealth, ecclesiastical and civil*, that is to say, of a political commonwealth with a theological foundation. The sentence – "that Jesus is the Christ" – recurs with the value of *leitmotif*, suggesting that this double structure is to be understood by analogy with the two natures of Jesus Christ. In the medieval conception of the king's two bodies, the state is at once both secular and divine. These two moments are represented on the title-plate of *Leviathan*. The state appears as an immense man, formed out of many small men. The common existence of all individuals is the super-human. Still for Hegel in the 19th century, the state is the "real God". Rousseau in the 18th century conceived the transformation of the many individual wills into the *volonté générale* as a numinosum. And he added to his treatise *The Social Contract*, the section on civil religion which – although at this stage purely posited – was needed to give the collective its binding force.

Rousseau was also deeply concerned, however, with the dissociative forces which come into play with this transformation of the individual to the collective subject. To the extent that the individual is not seamlessly absorbed into the body politic, it remains a disruptive moment. The general will fissures the particular will and gives it a schizoid-paranoid structure. Blanchot shows these dissociative tendencies and effects at work in *The Most High*. When Sorge becomes God at the end of Blanchot's novel, this false God shows up the delusional structures at work in the formation of the "real God" that is the State.

At the beginning of the *Social Contract*, in his lapidary formula, Rousseau defines the political domain in terms of a basic conflict of freedom and constraint.[27] "Man is born free, and everywhere he is in chains" (I,1, p. 45, 351.) Freedom is an essential determination of man, given to him by nature – he is "born free". The limitation of freedom, whether by a foreign power or by the social order, is not natural; it is one of the consequences of civilization and its founding convention. Rousseau refers to the

[27] Jean-Jacques Rousseau: *Du contrat social*, in: Jean-Jacques Rousseau: *Œuvres complètes*, III: *Du contrat social. Ecrits politiques*, edited by Bernard Gagnebin and Marcel Raymond, Paris, Gallimard, 1964 / *Discourse on Political Economy and The Social Contract*, translated by Christopher Betts. Oxford World Classics, 1994. This text is cited in parentheses with chapter and page-number; the first number referring to the English translation, and the second to the original French.

social order as a "holy law", forming the ground for all others. This sacral dimension of the political is not given by revelation; it is a result of convention. It arises when humans come together, and only exists as this convention; it thus becomes a second essential determination of the human, one that it is not natural, but supernatural: civilisation as a human construct. The sacral dimension develops when humans come together and form societies through conventions; it has a social and historical character. Within this supernatural space made up of the social and the sacral, the conventional and the historical, natural freedom becomes the dynamic moment. And this dynamic has an essentially agonal character.

Freedom is the nature and the essence of the human: its organon is the will. "To renounce our freedom is to renounce our character as men, the rights, and even the duties of humanity" (I, 4, p. 50, 387). Voluntary servitude is therefore an inherent contradiction. Nonetheless, voluntary subordination is the dynamic center of the social and the political. The convention is a con-volition, a co-ordination of wills. It is not voluntary servitude, but alienation of freedom for the sake of self-preservation. Freedom is the fire on the altar of the community; it is maintained through the self-sacrifice of the particular will as it transforms into the general will and establishes the institutional ground of the social. The sacral element of the political is constituted by this sacrificial transformation of the particular will.

Civil religion is the theological supplement to the political theory of the social contract. The political-theoretical understanding of the conversion of the particular will into the general will invests this process with a sacral meaning and makes it immanent. The political order is not theologically grounded, rather it becomes the sacred itself. The social bond – the *religio socialis* – is the "sacred right", introduced at the beginning of the treatise (I, 1, p. 46, 383). This right ratifies the "sacral name of the public good" (IV, 1, p. 135, 472); the entry into the social relation enacts the sacred bond of the polity and of the laws, and this bond is then expressed by civil religion. It is however a "purely civil profession of faith", and its articles are laid down by the sovereign; thus it is an institution based in convention (IV 8, p. 166, 503). The God here is the deistic divinity of the *philosophes*, the God that one would have to invent if he did not exist, as Voltaire says; the principle of the civil religion is the social order itself.

This transformation is the dynamic center of the social and of the political order. It is "the true foundation of society"; and makes a people into a people (I, 5, p. 54, 391). When the individual enters into the social order, it amounts to a transformation into a different mode of being, a "socialization". When the difficulties of self-preservation transcend the individual's forces, individuals have to unite their forces and act in concert. Force and freedom, originally moments belonging to the impulse for self-preservation in each individual, must then be put into play with and for others, in such a way that it is not harmful for the individual. The social order has to take on a form that will ensure that the collective force (*force commune*) protects the interests of the individual, so that in joining with all the others, each member of society continues only to obey himself and remains free. This is the essence of the social contract, which is not something that one really enters into, but which generates the structure of society, and hence the conditions for law and justice. The primary clause of the contract consists in the total alienation (*aliénation totale*) of each member, who hands over all his particular rights to the collective. This alienation is general and reciprocal: "each giving himself completely, the condition is the same for all" (I, 6, p. 55, 392). If this stipulation is not respected, then the individual returns to his initial freedom: *il reprend sa liberté naturelle.* This formula reappears as the central articulation of *The Most High*. It can now be understood as signifying the dysfunctional relation of particular and general, freedom and law. Rousseau shows that the antinomy of the political and of the law, as the agents of socialization, rests on this moment.

The *aliénation totale* of the individual in society is close to the point of confusion with the voluntary servitude, whose alienation – evoked with the same verb, *aliéner* – is said to be inhuman. The difference lies in the fact that in the process of entering society, the citizen gives his freedom over to all others, who for their part do the same: "Finally, each in giving himself to all gives himself to none" (I, 6, p. 55, 392). Nonetheless the proximity of this *aliénation* to that of servitude points to the fundamental conflict of the social and the political domains.

The total alienation signifies the transformation of the individual into a social being: sociality is another form, another mode of being of the person. It introduces the moment of the other into the personality: and this makes the personality structurally paranoid. Sociality is the paranoid element in the individual: it makes all others, and their interests, into a constitutive moment of the personality of the individual, the moment that is expressed in the general will. In this way, the social dimension constitutes an autonomous form of the mental life, which is at work not noetically, through the *nous*, but paranoetically, through the will. The socialized will, considered as a mental entity, as the organon of the intellect, introduces another form of thinking and knowing, one in which the paranoetic dimension is constitutive, since it necessarily and fundamentally implies consideration of other wills. The *aliénation totale* articulates the difference between the individual will and the other will as the general will.

In the social contract, the individual projects itself anew, now as a member of a society, a part of a whole, a citizen with responsibilities to every other individual within the total political body and to the political body as a whole. The personality of the citizen has different make-up from that of the individual, who has to make the citizen-being into the other part of his personality. Each other, as well as the totality of the others, become instances of a demand that is addressed to the individual – tendentially, they become his "persecutors". This structural moment in politics and society, right and law, and thus morality in general, is depicted in mythic thinking in the figure of the Erinyes.

The sacrifice of the particular will be involved in giving oneself over to all others is compensated by the reciprocity of the gift. The dynamic of giving and receiving creates a community as a new mode of human being: the sum of the assembled forces provides the increase in force that is needed to survive. By the alienation of all particular wills to all others, the particular will is transformed into the general will, creating a society as a new form of humanity. The sacrifice of the particular will is the medium through which the general will is formed. The transformation of all individuals creates a *corps moral et collectif*, in which every individual member becomes an inseparable part of the whole, whose unity is formed through this act of socialization. This "public person" has a "common I" and a life whose unity and existence is formed by the will, in just the same way as the individual.

A political form which prevents the realization of the social contract endangers the collective body. Thus particular political forms can be represented as forms of injury or sickness sustained by the social body, leading to pathological states in their citizens. Since the state has ontological status, it is a matter here of mental illnesses. Such vulnerability is already present on the elementary level constituted by the reciprocity of the social contract. The violation of the rights of any given individual is an injury to the collective body, which is immediately an injury to each one of its parts. Although each individual sacrifices his own particular will (*volonté particulière*) to the general (*volonté générale*) will as part of the founding act of socialization, he nonetheless retains his own will, and in particular cases this may deviate from the general will and even contradict it. Since the general will demands the total alienation of the particular will, the two instances are fundamentally opposed; it is here that we can locate the elemental conflict at the foundation of the political. The conflict between individual and citizen is continuously enacted in the individual in the guise of the conflict between the individual will of the *bourgeois* and the general will of the *citoyen*. The fact that the particular interests of the individual remain as an irreducible reality alongside the general interests of the general will inevitably leads to the injury of the body of the state; such a violation is constitutive for any political order. Rousseau makes this fundamental conflict very apparent, in using it to justify the right of the society to compel the individual to subjection under the general will – *on le forcera d'être libre* (I, 7, p. 58, 395). The *force commune* generated by the society created out of the general will becomes a violence turned against the individual, restricting the scope of the individual will. The conflict and the injury or illness that results defines the basic state of the political order.

The transition from the natural to the social condition, that is, the transformation of the particular will into the general will, of the individual into the citizen, introduces a new criteria of conduct. Actions are no longer oriented by drives (*instinct*), but by law and justice; they become moral, and law and reason overrule inclinations and wishes. With the transformation of natural freedom (*liberté naturelle*) into civil freedom (*liberté civile*), more sophisticated human qualities and abilities such as thinking, feeling and inner life develop (I, viii, 59, 396). These dimensions of human life unfold in the space of the difference between the two freedoms, the two wills (and *as* the space of this difference). Freedom and justice as the essence and the content of a higher humanity are marked by the conflictual relationship of the two wills.

The will as the instrument of freedom is its realization; it wills because it wills, without any kind of alienation or mediation. In its genuine realization, the will can exist as nothing other than its own action. Therefore the transposition of the particular will into the general will, if it is conceived as a total alienation, cannot be lasting or complete. By the very fact of being an individual will, it wants privilege (*préférence*), while as the general will, it wants equality (*égalité*). This inherent conflict between the particular will that has alienated itself and transformed itself into the general will, and the particular will, which as such can only will what is good for itself, remains a virulent element within the life of society, since the particular good is only contingently and occasionally identical with the general good, not essentially and permanently. The irreducible particularity in the will of the individual remains active as a dissident moment in the general will.

This constitution of the will implies that unconditional obedience to a political leader negates the existence of the collective. The command of the leader can only become the general will and have legal force when it is ratified by the general will as coinciding with the common good (II 1, p. 63-64, 400-401). If the collective obeys the commands of a leader when these run contrary to the general will and the common good, it leads to the destruction of the collective. The state and the political are "empty and deluding forms" when the particular prevails and presents itself under the mask of the universal (IV 1, p. 135, 472). In this situation, under the command of such a leader, the general will is alienated, de-viated from its natural rationality.

When the commands of the leader give voice to the collective, then they are legal and have legal force. The question, then, is what the universality of the collective is, and who belongs within it. For Rousseau, it is clear that this is a matter of a conventional decision. If scientific knowledge recognizes certain people as sub-human, then they are excluded from the sphere of universality. What at first appears to be a moral-ethical and juridical-political decision, which cannot be justified before the tribunal of the universal, is assured by scientific knowledge of race.

The general will engages the members of the community reciprocally. The individual acts in the medium of the general will for all others, but is also active on his own behalf at the same time. For with the word "everyone", each person thinks first of all of himself (II. 4, p. 405). The general will is based in human nature, in the tendency of each individual to give him or herself the preference. This inclination creates a structural aporia, which is supposed to lead to the transformation of self-interest into the general will. Such a metamorphosis will inevitably be precarious and labile, since its foundation – human nature and the individual will – is preserved as the motivation of the general will, in which everyone continues to think of himself. This fundamentally antinomic structure cannot be overcome. Hegel's solution is to conceive the individual will from the standpoint of reason; in this way, its nature as will becomes secondary and can be dismissed.

The general will is engaged in legislation; it is the will-principle of the collective, and the laws are its acts of will, giving concrete shape to the general will. Law and general will are correlative concepts. The purpose of laws is justice, which is the principle of the common good. Justice comes from God and is a universal rational principle. Since humans are not exclusively rational beings, they cannot immediately receive this principle from on high (*de si haut*); hence the will, the rational configuration of aspirations, passions, affects and desires, has to supplement the reason (II, 6, p. 73, 410). The laws are the expression of the general will: their object can only be the common good. In the law, the collective relates to itself by way of the power of its general will to accomplish the common good; the law is the collective itself, the expression of its will. Laws originating from the general will and having the common good as their purpose are by their nature just; the common good is the principle of justice. Here the deepest ground of the political order comes into view. The general will is necessarily general; the will of the individual is necessarily particular. The conflict of particular will and general will is played out in the citizen, in the form of the conflict between the law and self-interest. The individual will is criminal, rebellious and treacherous in relation to the general will, and so the individual, by virtue of his individual will, becomes the enemy of the collective; and conversely, the law becomes the enemy and the persecutor of the individual. The conflict of the individual and the general will makes up the tragic ground of the *polis*.

The political order is based on principles which are not accessible to it; it cannot reliably guarantee their maintenance in advance, because they are only formed with each realization of the general will. This performative is the sacral element of the political order. The realization takes place in the horizon of the common good: this common good, as the free decision of the general will, has to be ever realized anew, without the correctness of the decision ever being guaranteed. Undecidability becomes the principle of politics and justice, since it affects the principle of the common good, which has to accomplish the impossible equilibrium of the particular and the general will.

The theorists of German idealism seek to defuse this agonal conception of the political by reconciling the conflictual elements in the name of a higher reason and its idea. It remains a question, however, whether, as Hegel believed, Rousseau's analysis of the antinomy of the political is unphilosophical since it fails to grasp the true nature of freedom, or whether the idealist solution depends upon a surreptitious reconciliation. It may be that Hegel's pacification of the conflict restores a metaphysical truth, where Rousseau, in the mode of the Enlightenment, holds to an understanding of the universal as conventional and institutional.

Hegel's political philosophy is presented in the *Elements of a Philosophy of Right*: it represents one dimension of spirit (*Geist*).[28] The speculative center of this philosophy is the concept of freedom, which makes up the substance of right; the will is its organon. The system of right is "the realm of actualized freedom" and as a moment of the world of spirit, it is the "second nature" of humanity (§ 4). The will is free just as bodies have weight; freedom is only actual as will. Willing belongs within the practical domain, as opposed to the theoretical realm of thought. Where Rousseau defines the will beginning from the individual will, Hegel starts out from the "pure indeterminateness" of the pure will, not limited by any content. This willing of the will is a pure, content-less act: Hegel defines it as the self-relationality of the spirit. The will can therefore be determined as a particular mode of spirit, of which the essence is reason; and thus the antagonistic forces of the will can be reconciled by reason. Rousseau's conception, by contrast, would see the spirit as a particular mode of the will, and would allow its dynamic to unfold, rather than resolving its contradictions by reference to a higher instance.

For Hegel, pure willing is the negative side of freedom, which flees any kind of positive determination: it is the "freedom of the void" which "becomes in the realm of both politics and religion the fanaticism of destruction". The negative will is "absolute possibility"; hence it resists any kind of concrete realization. Its existence is "the fury of destruction" (§ 5). Since it is fundamentally anarchic, it is opposed to any kind of order; no state can be founded on this will. It has to be subordinated to reason, which transforms the anarchic-destructive moment into political order. Nonetheless, this "fury of destruction" remains for Hegel the elementary condition of the will. The question, then, is how destruction can be the "origin of becoming" (Sabina Spielrein). If the will is subordinate to reason, then the dialectical logic of the latter – corresponding to the dynamic of the conflict of ambivalence in psychoanalysis – can contain this destructive moment, and make it constructive. On the other hand, if Rousseau had in mind a con-

[28] Georg Wilhelm Friedrich Hegel: *Grundlinien der Philosophie des Rechts oder Naturrecht und Staatswissenschaft im Grundrisse* in: Georg Wilhelm Friedrich Hegel: *Werke*, Bd. 7, edited by Eva Moldenhauer and Karl Markus Michel, Frankfurt a. M., Suhrkamp, 1975 / *Elements in the Philosophy of Right*, translated by H.B. Nisbet, Cambridge, UP, 1991. This text is cited in parentheses referring to the number of the paragraph.

struction based in the dynamic of the will itself, then Hegel's refutation is unconvincing, since it does not operate on the same level.

The positive side of the will consists in the transition from pure indeterminateness to differentiation and the determination of a content. "I do not merely will, I will something" (§ 6). In this way, the I first becomes finite and particular, and attains real existence. The determinate I is contained in the indeterminateness of the will, which, however, is at first the universal over against this particularity. The "true infinite or concrete universality" is not given in the indeterminateness of the will; it is only produced with the concept. The tension of "immanent negativity" is that between indeterminacy and determinacy, between possibility and actuality, between infinity and finitude: this tension constitutes the I, inasmuch as it is will. If the work of the concept enacts this tension, then the concept, and thinking along with it, need to be conceived starting out from the structure of the will.

The will is the unity of the moments contained in this conflict. In wanting something, it makes the transition from universal to particular; but when it reflects on this process, it returns to the element of the universal. Thus the I posits itself as the "negative of itself"; it is determinate and limited in its universal identity. The I is "the self-reference of negativity" (§7). It knows, therefore, that determinateness is merely a non-binding possibility that it has itself posited. The freedom of the will consists in this knowledge: it is "the innermost insight of speculation, that is, infinity as self-referring negativity, this ultimate source of all activity, life, and consciousness". Freedom is the dynamic of the self-referring negativity: it is the innermost core of the spirit and of thought, since these have their ground in the will and its freedom. The "concrete concept of freedom" consists in being in the otherness of a determinate realization of freedom and yet at the same time, still remaining in oneself; thus, in being at once both determinacy and indeterminacy. Freedom does not lie in the obstinacy of wanting a certain particular thing, but rather in the willing that wants something determinate in the universal.

The concept of freedom provides the will with its purpose; an act of the will is the objectification of this purpose. It is limited by the content that is given when one wills something in particular, and by the formal articulation of the I and the object. At the outset, the will is subjective and its purpose is identified with *my* freedom, with the freedom of the particular individual. Hegel reveals the inadequacy of this moment, which needs to be elevated into the domain of spirit by the process of speculative knowledge. The will comes to recognize that its freedom is real, not in the subjective sphere, but in the objective and universal sphere. If the wilfulness of the particular individual is fundamental and constitutive, as Rousseau assumes, however, then it will remain irreducible on the level of reality, for all that it may be transcended in speculative thought. It is questionable then, if the initial articulation of the will that consists in the "self-reference of negativity" and which is, as such, a basic component of the speculative process, is really resolved into "the Idea, this real God" (§ 258), or if this is merely a construction, artificially introduced in order to bring the process to an end.

The self-reflection of the will leads it to understand that it only truly wills when it objectively realizes its freedom; this moment comes about with the law. The pure potentiality of the will, its absolute possibility as a freedom to do anything at all, is the genuine core of freedom. Any given determinate realization is a limitation upon this absolute possibility and "does not belong to the essence of freedom itself" (§ 10). But since the realization of freedom is the purpose of the will, it has to go beyond this moment of the particular limitation, and realize the absolute possibility in objective form. The system of the law is such a realization of the absolute possibility of freedom. The meaning of the will is the realization of freedom; the purpose of history is progress in the consciousness of freedom. The realization of freedom takes place with the law, and with the state. Therefore, an adequate theory of law and politics has to be based in a theory of the will, as the instrument of freedom.

The natural and immediate will is spontaneous; it wills in accord with its inclinations and desires, and these, for Hegel, already belong to the rational dimension of the will. The content of the desire is "rational in itself, but expressed in so immediate a form, it does not yet have the form of rationality" (§ 11). They still need to be politically and legally configured in accord with the idea of freedom; thus, in order that the will become truly rational, it has to be socialized and politicized.

The object of thought is universal and infinite. The universality and infinity of the will is what is properly mine; it belongs to the individual. However, the individual has to recognize itself as in fact finite, despite its apparent infinitude, and to spiritualize itself through thought in the "work of freedom" in order to attain to "free universality"; in this way, the individual becomes an "objective, infinite will" (§ 13). If thinking and will relate to each other as universal and individual, infinite and finite, then the conflict which Rousseau identifies at the basis of socialization in terms of an antinomy of the particular and the general will, becomes in Hegel the basis of the mental state. The conflict of the psychonoetic faculties will and reason, the subjective inclination and objectively rational will, makes up the deep structure of law and politics, the order of the polis. This conflict is resolved by Hegel, in transforming the bad infinity of the will into the true infinity of reason.

Rousseau had shown that the principle of the will is opposed to any such resolution, and makes a complete transformation impossible. Hegel's analysis shows that for the will as absolute possibility every realization is only one possibility among others. The will-self is essentially the possibility to choose (§ 14). The content is necessary to the will; but the determinate content is merely possible in any given case (§ 15). Every individual choice is arbitrary and contingent; the essence of the free action of the will is the element of contingency contained in the decision. This freedom of arbitrariness becomes true freedom through the self-reflection of the will; this takes place concretely in the creation of customs, laws and rights. Nonetheless the moment of arbitrariness, the "abstract certainty on the part of the will as to its freedom", remains irreducible; the abstract certainty of freedom as absolute possibility is in conflict with the truth of the will as the idea of freedom.

In itself, the free will is subjective; but when it is realized, in and for itself, it becomes objective will. The core of the subjective will is the pure I, which only has itself as object, abstracted from all content. "Thus, subjectivity may have wholly particular significance, or it may mean something eminently justified, since everything which I am to recognize also has the task of becoming mine and gaining its validity in me. Such is the infinite greed of subjectivity, which collects and consumes everything within this simple source of the pure I" (§ 26). This longing of subjectivity is the antagonistic moment; if it is "eminently justified", then it is also a form of the infinite and the universal that is realized as law. The "infinite greed" is the subjective part of the law.

This conflict of pure wilfulness and the consciousness of the common good is to be overcome in the self-reflection of the will, which allows it to see that the freedom of arbitrariness always remains merely particular. Thus self-will is sacrificed on the altar of the general will. When the rational good is the object of the will, then the individual acts "not as a particular individual, but in accordance with the concepts of ethics in general: in an ethical act I vindicate not myself but the thing [*die Sache*]" (§ 15). The natural man, with his instincts and desires, is the negative, which is to be "eradicated" (§ 18). He has to become a citizen, and transform his human being into citizen being. Hegel's argument has its starting point in the idea of freedom and of the law. Any element of the particular is merely something that has still to be elevated into the element of spirit (*Geist*). By contrast, for Rousseau, who argues from an anthropological standpoint, the residual particularity is irreducible, not something that has to be "eradicated".

The contradictions that arise between the multiplicity of the instincts does not lead to a "dialectic of instincts and inclinations" (§ 17). This only takes place through the mediation of the Idea, which represents the higher instance into which the contradictions resolve. But if the ambivalence of the drives and the affects is a fundamental moment of the will, one that is decided only by the arbitrariness of the subjective decision, then it has to be elevated into the domain of the spirit; it has to assume a form proper to this realm and be given its function in the idea of freedom that for Hegel constitutes the truth of the will. Truth as freedom then necessarily acquires the character of ambivalence: and this ambivalence develops, not as a dialectic of drives, but rather as the transformation of the ambivalent dynamic of drives into a dialectic; and this leads to deconstruction as a form of thought.

The realization of freedom purifies the drives of their natural determinations, leading them to their substantial essence as the "the rational system of the will's determination" (§ 19). For Hegel, this rationality is not that of the drives and the will themselves. The will has to bring itself into accord with reason: reason is the principle of the domain of spirit. Thus it needs to be cleansed of the "crudity and barbarity" of its instinctual basis (§ 20). If the will is the instrument of freedom, however, then the determination of freedom, and of the law as the realization of freedom, must be grounded in the structure of the will and proceed from it. The ambivalence of the instincts and the "self-referring negativity" will necessarily provide the dominant moment of the structure of freedom and the law. Hence Derrida can argue that "deconstruction is justice".[29]

Hegel explicitly conceives his *Philosophy of Right* as a critique of Rousseau. The latter does not understand the will as inherently rational, as the "true Spirit", but as individual: in Rousseau, "the substantial basis and primary factor…is will and spirit as the particular individual, as the will of the single person in his distinctive arbitrariness" (§ 29). For this initial will, the claims of reason are merely an obstacle. For Hegel, however, reason is to be seen as the genuine realization of the freedom and the will. Here we see the speculative version of the concept of freedom. The antinomy of the law that Rousseau reveals, which places the individual person and the citizen in an irreconcilable

[29] Jacques Derrida: *Force de loi. Le "Fondement mystique de l'autorité"*, Paris, Galilée, 1994 / *Force of Law*, *The Cardozo Law Review* 11, 1989-1990, p. 945, 30.

tension, leads to the bad infinity of freedom. Hegel's resolution of this antinomy, on the other hand, leads to the genuine freedom. But if the antinomy of man and citizen, self-will and collective will is inherent in the structure of the will – and Hegel's "justified" subjectivity points in this direction – then the "totality of the system of law" (§ 28) is actually totalitarian and the opposite of freedom. It institutes the system of universal freedom only through the sacrifice of the particular freedom. The eradication of the particular is the terror of reason. The opposition of Hegel and Rousseau is itself antinomic; it is the conflict of the particular and the universal.

This conflict is not accidental but essential. The accidental element, the contingency of the particular will, with its arbitrariness and its "infinite greed", is a substantial part of the law. As an essential, absolute and incalculable chance element, it cannot be integrated into the "totality of the system of the law", and remains a disruptive moment. This can be understood on two levels. The decisions of the individual can be seen as inaccessible to reason, because they are not rational or rule-governed, but voluntary and free. Derrida cites Kierkegaard from the supplement to the third chapter of the *Philosophical Fragments*: "The moment of decision is a madness. "[30] "Madness does not make rights", Rousseau states categorically in *The Social Contract* (I, 4, p. 50, 387). The ethically demanding decision of the individual is the point at which the will of the individual is articulated with the general will. Because its consequences are unforeseeable, such a decision takes place within the horizon of non-knowledge. The futural dimension of the decision makes up part of its intractability. But the individual is also a disruptive moment for the systematic interpretation of law to the extent that it represents an absolute and intractable other. It is not a question now of the "wilfulness" of the individual will and its freedom, but of the particularity of the other, in his or her freedom. From this point of view, the particular will stands opposed, not to the general will, but to the other individual will. Freedom, then, becomes the articulation of two wills.

For Hegel, on the other hand, the ethical life is the unity of the will. "Personal aloofness", he writes, is first overcome by love and sensibility, which absorb it into the whole of the family. Civil society then forms a whole that is held together "only by the bond of mutual need". The state, as ethical life and spirit, is the third stage, within which "the momentous unification of self-sufficient individuality with universal substantiality takes place". When right appears in the form of the state it is "freedom in its most concrete shape" (§ 33). "The state is the actuality of the ethical Idea" (§ 257). It is "rational in and for itself" and "an absolute and unmoved end in itself, and in it, freedom enters into its highest right". Thus, it is the unity of universal knowledge and particular activity. "Rationality [...] consists in the unity of objective freedom (i.e. of the universal substantial will) and subjective freedom (as the freedom of individual knowledge and of the will in its pursuit of particular ends)." Rousseau was the first to recognize "the will as the principle of the state" and to have thought the individual will in relation to the general will; but he regarded "the universal will not as the will's rationality in and for itself, but only as the common element arising out of this individual will as a conscious will". As a contract, which proceeds from the union of the individual wills, this "common element" is based in arbitrary individual will, and not substantial

[30] Jacques Derrida: *Force de loi. Le "Fondement mystique de l'autorité"*, Paris, Galilée, 1994 / *Force of Law*, *The Cardozo Law Review* 11, 1989-1990, p. 967, 58.

freedom. In contrast, "the objective will is rational in itself, whether or not it is recognized by individuals and willed by them at their discretion" (§ 258). Thus, instead of the rationality of the will becoming the principle of socialization, the "eminently justified" particularity of the will is "eradicated" in the name of rationality.

The state is the realization of freedom, and as such, "the absolute end of reason". Thus it is Spirit (*Geist*), which realizes itself in the world with consciousness. This consciousness is not that of the individual, but objective consciousness, realizing itself as "a self-sufficient power": "The state consists of the march of God in the world, and its basis is the power of reason actualizing itself as will." Here it is not a matter of any particular state, but "the Idea, this actual God" (§ 258). The power of the state is that of reason as the supreme principle.

When Hegel criticizes Rousseau's political theory as unphilosophical, he has in view Rousseau's conception of the will in terms of "the will of the single person [*des Einzelnen*] in his distinctive arbitrariness"; such an approach is "devoid of any speculative thought" and remains in the empirical realm of "the particular individual" (§ 29). The philosophical concept of the will, by contrast, is concerned with the "rational will which has being in and for itself". Hegel here distorts the reality of the will, as one can see if one considers the history of the concept. The concept of the will, as a mental faculty alongside and distinct from reason, begins to develop in late antiquity and its speculative dimension is progressively worked out within Christianity.[31] Hegel, like Rousseau, starts out from the will as the instrument of praxis, and makes it into a basic element of a political theory, but he conceives it first and last from the standpoint of reason, and in view of the accomplishment of reason: in other words, not as will. The *Elements of the Philosophy of Right* remain therefore – philosophy. Hegel orients the will and the freedom which is essentially given with it in the direction of "the idea, this real god".

A rigorous conception of will, however, needs to take its point of departure in freedom, and the decision that is bound up with it. The will is the organon of the decision made in the element of freedom. Kierkegaard describes the moment of decision as madness, because it is occasional by its nature, and made on the basis of criteria that one has instituted oneself. The power of the will provides the dynamic for such a crisis: in the morally demanding decision, it forms the power of judging between good and evil. The problem of evil belongs together with such a free choice. The freedom of the will is the space of possibility for a decision. Hence the structure of the will is essentially double; this divided condition comes back to the decision between good and evil. The free will is the instance of the crisis of good and evil.

The profoundly ambiguous and agonal conception of the will that results is placed by Rousseau at the center of his political theory. His conception of the will is not at all empirical; he reveals its speculative dimension in making the constitutive division of the will into its essential principle. Since Hegel treats the will according to the univocal logic of the concept in the field of reason, and thus defines it as "true Spirit" (*Geist*), he can conceive of the subjective as the "particular individual" and "the will of the single person [*des Einzelnen*] in his distinctive arbitrariness" as transcended in the absolute of

[31] See: Gerhard Poppenberg: *Antike oder Moderne? Altes und Neues zum freien Willen*, in: *Philosophische Rundschau* 58 (2012), p. 259–273.

the Idea. If law and right are the forms of the rational universal, of the universal as reason, the agon of the will appears as a mark of the deficient subjectivity, the subjectivity that is not yet purified in the absolute of the concept and the Idea.

By contrast, Rousseau defines the will as the organon of subjectivity in such a way that it constitutes two modes of being, the two natures of the individual as human being and as citizen. The agon that thus arises between freedom and obligation, as the individual and universal aspects of the human being, is not overcome in being taken up in to the absolute of the law. Rather, it forms the deeply ambiguous nature of the law and the truth of the political order that is regulated by it. The freedom of the individual and its will "in its distinctive arbitrariness" is therefore not merely an empirical, but an ontological category. Freedom is essentially particular, and likewise, the particular being is essentially freedom. And this essential freedom of the individual cannot be integrated into the absolute of the idea, since it is the unbound element of the will, the free decision such as it is made at any given moment. An adequate political theory would have to take this ambiguous and unreliable dimension of the will as the foundation of a conception of law, right and justice. Right is not therefore "something utterly sacred" as the genuine existence of the concept (§ 30): rather as the *opus operatum* of socialization, which is carried out in the self-sacrifice of the individual in the field of the agon between particular and general will.

One can indeed wonder how such an agonistic dynamic of the will could give rise to a universal that would go beyond the conventionality of the contract, which Hegel rightly criticizes as depending on the majority of those coming together, and not on the matter itself. When right originates in convention, it can assume a different aspect with each new convention that is enacted. Hegel underlines the devastating consequences of this conception: the "fearfulness" of *Realpolitik*, the perversion of power that characterized the revolutionary Terror (§ 29). He countered this danger with the absolute of the Idea, against which every particular viewpoint has to measure itself, with which all such viewpoints have to bring themselves into accord. But the question remains if there is a universal, which is not only quantitatively, but also qualitatively grounded in the dynamic of the will, and that will emerges from out of this dynamic. The will is the organon of the good, not the true; it is not an agent of knowledge, but rather of action. Hence it is situational and occasional. It is questionable, then, if there can be any criterion that would give an absolute for the decision in the moment, which is occasional, ever different.

Blanchot only rarely participated in the political debates of the post-war period. But in 1984, he published a reflection on the question of the political in the journal, *Le Débat*. The text explores the figure of the intellectual and the role of this figure in the public sphere. A prefatory remark signals the incompleteness of the remarks. "The intellectuals in question" was nonetheless published without modifications as a book in 1996, since it sketches out essential questions.[32] It situates itself in opposition to a position

[32] Maurice Blanchot: *The Intellectuals in Question*, in: *The Blanchot Reader*. Edited by Michael Holland. London: Blackwell, 1995/ *Les Intellectuels en Question: Ébauche d'une réflexion* in: *Le Débat* 29 (1984) and Paris, Fourbis, 1996. Page numbers in parenthesis refer first to the English version and then to the French version in its book form.

represented by the name of Lyotard.[33] The intellectual of the late 20th century can no longer, as in the Enlightenment, stand for a "general idea", since we have come to recognize to what extent reason is grounded in un-reason, and that the use of reason also sets free the powers of un-reason. The result was a refusal of universal claims of reason. Psychoanalysis approaches the question by exploring how a "rational society" can be constructed on the irrational foundation of the unconscious by way of the sublimation and spiritualization of the instinctual basis into cultural acts and social activity – allowing that the form of the sublimations cannot be dictated in advance: it also considers what it means for reason that it is grounded in unreason (p. 206, 8-9). The question of an irrational ground of reason and of a "rational society" becomes only more enigmatic and uncanny when Blanchot names the attraction of fascism as "the irrational", which he glosses as "the power of spectacle and a hybrid resurgence of certain forms of the sacred" as well as the desire of society for myths (p. 220, 49).

In Blanchot's conception, the intellectual is not the poet, the philosopher or the artist, the historian or the scholar, but "part of ourselves"; it is the instance of the world in general which demands at certain moments that the intellectual turns away from his own tasks, in order to judge the events that are taking place; it is the instance of the citizen in the human being. The intellectual stands on the border of the particularity of the task and the generality of the events taking place in the world. In turning towards the world, he or she becomes visible as an intellectual. This does not imply an immediate participation in events, or the exercise of personal power, but rather an action within a reserved space. The intellectual is removed from the political sphere, without having actively retreated from it, in a proximity that is also a distance. His "active attentiveness" is less an expression of a "care of the self" than a "care for others" (p. 208, 13).

The intellectual observes and meditates on the political order. He is not therefore defined by his intelligence as a specialist for the general. Valéry had already dispensed the intellectual from direct action, assigning him to the realm of the word. The intellectual *says* what is true and just, not as a theoretician, but at the liminal point in between theory and praxis (p. 209, 15). He takes sides, in accordance with the reasons that for him are the most important. In a time in which the universal has fallen into disrepute, seen as "the untrue", and as totalitarian, he nonetheless keeps in view a general and a universal. The measure of this universal is the "care for others". The universal idea has its foundation in the privilege of the other.

The origin and the foundation of the modern intellectual, not only as a just cause, but as the cause as such, was the Dreyfus affair. It showed that the naturally solitary intellectuals can act collectively when their cause is at stake, in an "individualist universalism" (p. 210, 18). The cause here is justice: "a universal idea of what is just and what is unjust" (p. 210, 19). The intellectuals, as individuals, are aristocrats of the spirit, but when it is a matter of the cause, they become democrats of justice (p. 210, 20). Justice is

[33] Jean-François Lyotard: *Tombeau de l'intellectuel et autres essais*, Paris, Galilée, 1984. He defines the intellectual as one who acts in accordance with a universal value. Since thought has lacked such a "totalizing unity or universality" since the 19th century, the figure of the intellectual has become extinct. "One can only be an intellectual without forfeiting one's honour if the injustice is not shared, if the victims are only victims, and the executioners are unforgivable" (p. 11, 16-17).

the *causa efficiens* and the *causa finalis,* the cause and the purpose for the intellectuals, because it is general in a double sense: as justice in itself, and as justice for all – and not in the Hegelian style, justice in and for itself, the identification of right and state. The distance from Hegel underlines the difference between a true and a false universal; the latter is perverted to the precise extent that it makes common cause with the state, and identifies justices with right, and only with right. Such an inverted universal allows no counter-instance; or more precisely, it contains no such instance, having excluded or superseded it. This is why the Dreyfus affair is of such fundamental importance. The anti-Semitism of the affair situated the task of the intellectual in connection with "the Jewish question" and imposed "a simple demand":"the demand for truth and justice, the call for freedom of the mind against fanatic vehemence" (p. 212, 23).

Blanchot returns several times to mark an important distinction. The intellectual cannot stand on the side of the absolute, of the holy: he cannot be a cleric, a substitute for a priest. This leads to the distinction between the universal and the absolute, between justice and law. It is a matter here of thinking a universal that does not have absolute character, and nonetheless is binding; the compelling power of the universal here cannot overrule the unbound nature that determines the intellectual. The intellectual has to consider the cause of justice as a universal, which is at all times the end – *la fin des fins* – and never the means to some other political purpose (p. 214, 30). The question cannot be, as it was for the socialists, whether Dreyfus is poor or rich, but only if justice is at stake in his case.

The task of the intellectual is to maintain the "simple idea of justice" against any kind of political judgment or class-interest – "a justice as abstract and formal as the idea of man in general can be" (p. 215, 33). The universal idea of humanity begins with the individual; that is the accomplishment of the French revolution, which "would make applicable the finest of principles, which would revolutionize humanity" (p. 209, 17). The Dreyfus affair is fundamental for the intellectual because of its roots in anti-Semitism. Therefore it is compatible for Blanchot with the other anti-Semitic "affair" and gives the measure for the conduct of the intellectual with regard to National Socialism. The point of the parallel lies in the attitude of the intellectuals in the two cases. Dreyfusards and anti-fascists act in the same spirit. The Resistance becomes the site and the movement of the intellectuals in the 1940s.

Since the Resistance is also a military engagement, Blanchot adds an excursus on the problem of war, which leads into the center of his conception of the political. Proletarian socialism always saw the liberation of the workers as an act of war. The idea of preparing and accelerating revolutions through wars has implications that lead beyond socialism: "For the decisive character of justice (justice for others) is that it brooks no delay, so that as a consequence it can let slip no opportunity – be it dangerous or doubtful – to fulfil itself" (p. 219, 45). "Justice cannot wait": Derrida will pick up this central affirmation.[34] The spirit of justice has a tendency to impatience, which can lead to dangerous lines of thought and actions: to murder and to wage war in the name of justice.

Blanchot illustrates the theological deep structure of this figure of thought with a citation from Martin Buber's *Gog and Magog*. Here Buber tells of a 19th century rabbi

[34] Jacques Derrida: *Force de loi. Le "Fondement mystique de l'autorité"*, Paris, Galilée, 1994 / *Force of Law*, *The Cardozo Law Review* 11, 1989-1990, p. 967, 57.

who had considered whether Napoleon was a figure of *demonic power*, and if by the excess of evil that he represented, he could hasten the arrival of the Messiah. This leads to the "riskiest of questions": "ought one to promote Evil, bring it to a paroxysm, and hence precipitate catastrophe, so that at the same time deliverance may draw nearer. Couched in religious terms, this is the controversy which will, in the twentieth century, prove the great intellectual dispute, and which goes on today, in a form which only appears to be new" (p. 220, 46). Christianity had already posed the same question, in the wake of the second of Paul's Letters to the Thessalonians. Should one resist the appearance of the anti-Christ and oppose to it the state-order as the katechontic principle or should one promote the arrival of the anti-Christ, since it precedes the return of Christ. In the political dimension, following Blanchot's commentary on the French revolution, this would correspond to the question of the – apparent – necessity of terror and barbarism "so as to make applicable the finest of principles which would revolutionize humanity" (p. 209, 17).

The form this mythical agon could take in "the great intellectual dispute" of the twentieth century appears in Blanchot's analysis of National Socialism and the Resistance. The fascination exercised by fascism, at the expense of democracy, stemmed from its irrational and mythic dimension. Hitler's struggle against the Jews had its foundation in the essence of Judaism itself, in its monotheism and its renunciation of images. Judaism signified "a rejection of myths, a forswearing of idols, the recognition of an ethical order manifesting itself in respect for the Law" (p. 221, 50). The Jew as "freed from myth" represents a counter-figure to the fascist. Taken together, fascism and Judaism illustrate the opposition of idolatrous mythos and imageless law. To the extent that it articulates the demand for justice, the law itself nonetheless has a mythic ground, as Blanchot shows with reference to the constellation of good and evil. The antagonism of good and evil, as conceived in the mythical-theological tradition, has its counterpart in the conflictual relationship of reason and unreason. Just as reason and the "rational society" have an irrational foundation, right and justice have a mythical foundation.

For this reason, Blanchot takes the mythic structure as the basis of his analysis of the politics of the 1930s. The anti-fascist Resistance was confronted with the question of war from the beginning. With the occupation of the Rhineland, at the latest, the question of military intervention was pressing. The intellectuals became pacifists, when they should have become militant and supported the French government in their plans for counter-attack. Anti-fascism abdicated, in order not to imitate Hitler. The pacifism of the 1930s was the error of the intellectuals, their guilt with respect to their historical task of supporting the militant movement. The problem became acute with the Resistance to the Occupation. The aporia of these remarks is evident. The pacifist intellectuals make themselves guilty by their non-engagement; the engaged intellectuals who join the Resistance become guilty by the evil means that they deploy in order to struggle for the good.

The outcome of these reflections is that there is finally no objective criterion that would decide for or against the engagement of the intellectual, only the demand of the universal ideas of justice and freedom – without any kind of guarantee that these ideas will not themselves be travestied in the engagement. The fact that justice is characterized as a demand makes it into a task. The status of the universal idea is precarious; freedom and justice are universal demands, but not objective givens that could define a starting point. They only become real when they are put into practice. The intellectual embodies the demand of an action which cannot take its orientation from any point that is fixed in advance: there is no criterion for decision beyond the demand itself, which is compelled to create its frame of reference through its own activity.

The Resistance illustrated this dilemma, since it showed the need for a struggle for freedom and justice, and the need to take decisions that could place hostages or civilians at risk. It was not always possible to confine means and ends within desirable limits; excess was at times necessary (p. 222, 54). The demand for justice and freedom was confronted with the problem of what becomes of "the good (the liberation of the peoples)" when the means to its attainment is "the evil (war)". Robespierre recognized immediately that the revolution is corrupted by war, since the good is altered when it is attained through evil; it is contaminated, and can even become malevolent; the good that was in it is broken, corrupted. This argument belongs with the horizon of Camus' merciless critique of revolution as war, which needs terror to maintain itself. Nothing can guarantee that the evil means will not definitively ruin the good ends. We no longer have the assurance of Christian theodicy, where the guarantee of the good is given with God, who has providentially ordered the course of the world such that everything comes out well in the end. There is only the *demand* for justice and freedom and the imperative stated by Adorno: to act in such a way that Auschwitz will not be repeated. The task of the intellectual is to ask the old question – whether there are good reasons for the evil – under modern conditions, the conditions named by Lukács as "transcendental homelessness".

A final problem is the legitimacy of the intervention of the intellectuals, who make use of an influence that they have attained in a specialized domain, and extend it to other purposes. This derived, transferred authority raises problems analogous to the relation of good and evil: nothing guarantees that the authority of the intellectual will not be corrupted in its exercise in the political sphere. For Blanchot, the conclusion to be drawn is that to be an intellectual is not a position that one can occupy permanently, but only ever in relation to a particular cause. Moreover, the intellectual does not stand up for the cause alone, but only in joining with others. The determinate cause has its measure in the universal cause. The task of the intellectual is to judge the determinate cause in the horizon of the universal demand, and to act accordingly. But the danger always remains that the balance between means and ends, war and liberation, good and evil is lost (p. 224, 59).

Blanchot does not discuss in any further detail whether the intellectual, who tends towards an anonymous and collective mode of being, also has a relation to guilt, in addition to the relation to evil risked in speaking out for a political cause. Instead, he cites a passage from René Char dating back to the year 1943, which gives the struggles of that time a mythic dimension; this is the same year in which Blanchot had discussed the question of an "innocence inside evil" in his essay on the Orestes myth: "I want never to forget that I have been forced to become – for how long? – a monster of justice and intolerance, a cooped-up simplifier, an arctic individual with no interest in the fate of anyone who is not in league with him to kill the hounds of hell" (p. 225, 62).[35]

[35] René Char: *Recherche de la base et du sommet*, in: René Char: *Œuvres complètes*, Paris, Gallimard, p. 633.

The intellectual is the figure of the differentiation between good and evil. He or she makes a decision, not from any absolute standpoint, but in view of a universal – the idea of the human and the demand of justice for all – that is to be realized on the basis of this differentiation. In a given situation, the intellectual makes an objection in the name of justice, and speaks for those who suffer injustice. As an advocate in this sense, speaking from a position that is not bound to any specific party the intellectual becomes the figure of the sovereign; he or she makes the decisive call, saying what is right, what is just. This call is only made in the situation as it is given, and only for this situation – but nonetheless, it is made in view of the universal of justice, and expresses the *exigence universelle* – to act in a particular cause in accordance with the universal cause. Because this universal – the idea of humanity and justice – is still to be realized, it belongs to the future; it is the task that arises from the ever renewed universal demand of an articulation between the determinate cause and the universal cause.

Blanchot's reflections take on a clearer profile in the horizon of discourse on the intellectual published by Julien Benda in 1927 – *La Trahison des Clercs* (The Treason of the Intellectuals).[36] For Benda, the intellectual is a *clerc* – a cleric, someone who has turned away from the world, whether it be as a churchman, a philosopher, a writer, an artist or a scientist, and who now speaks out against the passions of the world in the name of justice and humanity. The "betrayal" of the title refers to the abandonment of the "eternal values" in favour of direct action. The moral prestige and the authority which the intellectual has acquired through his or her activity in an extra-worldly dimension is put into the service of an activity within the world. For Benda, the Dreyfus Affair was the occasion of this shift. Zola's *J'accuse* is not an abstract call for justice; it concerns this particular case. The "spiritual office" of the intellectual is now bound up with a particular cause. The intellectual is no longer a "cleric", committed to the good in general, but a politician representing a particular cause.[37]

As a cleric, the intellectual represents the "abstract quality of the human", without acting in the interest of any concrete purpose (p. 81). The criterion of the betrayal for Benda, therefore, is that thinking and knowledge become historical; the intellectual no longer occupies the realm of the eternal and the immutable, but that of becoming and of history. The historicization of thought, however, is the mark of modern age since the Enlightenment. The original sin of the modern intellectual is to have fallen from the sphere of the eternal and the ideal into the historical and real sphere of politics. Benda

[36] Julien Benda: *La trahison des clercs*, Paris, Grasset, 1975 (^{1}1927; ^{2}1946) / *The Treason of the Intellectuals*, translated by Richard Aldington, New York, Norton, 1969. References with page-number in parenthesis.

[37] In a 1928 book review, Walter Benjamin attested to Benda's "strictly reactionary intellectual attitude". See: Walter Benjamin: *Drei Bücher: Viktor Schklowski, "Sentimentale Reise durch Rußland"; Alfred Polgar, "Ich bin Zeuge"; Julien Benda: "Der Verrat der Intellektuellen"*, in: Walter Benjamin: *Gesammelte Schriften*, Band III: *Kritiken und Rezensionen*, Edited by Hella Tiedemann-Bartels, Frankfurt a. M., Suhrkamp, 1972, p. 112. Georges Bataille cites Jean Wahl's principle, according to which anyone who esteems Benda as a philosopher and thinker can himself not be considered a philosopher or thinker. See: Georges Bataille: *Giraud – Pastoureau – Benda – Du Moulin de Laplante – Govy*, in: Georges Bataille: *Œuvres complètes*, Vol. XI, Paris, Gallimard, 1988, p. 191.

insists on a strict separation between the realm of spirit and the ideal, on the one hand, and that of politics and power, on the other. This "division of functions" is "the presupposition for culture" (p. 139). The intellectual cannot conflate free thinking with the practical, goal-directed mode of thought that is proper to action in the world. In becoming a political actor, the intellectual fails to fulfil the office of "protecting the flame of the non-practical values" (p. 159). He or she becomes a citizen and disappears as an intellectual.

Lyotard draws the same conclusion from the movement of modern thought: but he derives it from this very modernization itself. Since modern thought historicizes thinking, it makes it impossible to stand up for eternal values. In this light, Blanchot's conception of the intellectual appears as an attempt to save a universal under the conditions of the modern age, and in its wake, without being reactionary and reverting to the eternal. For Benda, justice, as a non-instrumental value, cannot become a principle of action; "it is static, not dynamic", he writes in the preface to the 1946 edition. Historical praxis unfolds "on the field of injustice" (p. 78). Blanchot defines the intellectual as the agent of a dynamic process of the realization of justice. Since the intellectual stands between theory and praxis, he or she moves "in the field of injustice" and becomes a "monster of justice". The realization of justice always takes place within a horizon of possible injustice, and in certain cases, it has to make injustice into a means for justice, in order "to kill the hounds of hell". Such is the lot of the modern intellectual; the moment of betrayal is unavoidable if justice is to be done.

With the evocation of Buber's book *Gog and Magog* (1943), Blanchot places the intellectual in the eschatological constellation of the final struggles (Ez 38/39; Rev 20) and thus gives a mythological and theological deep-structure to the question of justice. The struggle for justice in any given present situation takes place in view of these struggles "at the end of time" (Ez 38,16): it is from these struggles that the universal discloses itself. The crisis of good and evil is thus conceived within the terms of the eschatological allegory of the final struggle.

Jacques Derrida engages with the implications of this reflection in his essay, "The Force of Law".[38] The philosopher formalizes Blanchot's agonal mythic figure of thought, and makes it into an argument concerning the philosophy of right (although he does not engage with the problematic of will). Derrida begins with a remark of Pascal's on the reciprocal relationship of justice and force. Justice and right require force in order to impose themselves; but force also needs justice, in order not to become tyrannical or terrorist. Derrida comments: "Justice demands, as justice, recourse to force. The necessity of force, then, is implied in the *juste* in *justice*" (p. 937, 23). The conventional reading interprets Pascal's thought to mean that law and right are not inherently just; they are just only because they prevail as laws, because they are invested with authority and imposed with violence. Derrida, however, drawing on a formula of Montaigne cited by Pascal, seeks to unearth the "mystical foundation of authority", and thus to reject the notion that the constellation of justice and force simply refers back to the right of the strongest. His aim is a fundamental "critique of juridical authority, a de-sedimentation

[38] Jacques Derrida: *Force de loi. Le "Fondement mystique de l'autorité"*, Paris, Galilée, 1994 / *Force of Law*, *The Cardozo Law Review* 11, 1989-1990. Page references in parentheses are first to the English, then to the French version.

of the legal superstructure" (p. 941, 25). Such an ideology-critique of the notion of right intends to show how it is constituted as right, and how it functions. The establishment of right through force or violence also implies an interpretive force/violence: a particular right is established in the interests of those who make the law. This interpretive and therefore linguistic dimension of the initial legislation links language with force/violence; it reveals signification as violence and violence as signification.

Force/violence is a constitutive moment of law and justice, not a power external to them. The founding and justifying moment of law and justice "would consist of a *coup de force*, of a performative and therefore interpretive violence that is in itself neither just nor unjust and that no justice and no previous law with its founding anterior moment could guarantee or contradict or invalidate". This performative force/violence is the limit of discourse. Derrida designates it as "the mystical", explicating the term in a sentence whose cryptic character mirrors the thing itself: "Here a silence is walled up in the violent structure of the founding act. Walled up, walled in, because silence is not exterior to language" (p. 943, 28).

The origin of authority and the institution of the law have no external supporting instance and can only be based on themselves. It is a violence without foundation, a groundless and abyssal violence – an *acte gratuite* – "neither legal nor illegal" (p. 943, 29). The foundation of the law is a self-foundation, and remains suspended above an abyss of force/violence. Violence is inherently anomic: and it is also part of *nomos*, which is therefore divided by an inner antinomy. Violence is the other of the law as part of the law, that which, in the law, is not the law. Violence is the separated and alien constituent, which the law has to integrate back into itself; it is the reprehensible part which cannot simply be repudiated, since otherwise, it returns as the phantasm in the real, in accordance with the logic of psychosis. The law is absolutely without justification and groundless: but this unfounded ground is justice, which is the performative force/violence of its own institution. The unfounded ground is active in every legal judgement as its deep structure; it is the mystical limit of every morally demanding decision, the final unjustifiability of the decision, which therefore takes place over an abyss of madness (to apply the terms of Kierkegaard's remark from the third chapter of the *Philosophical Fragments*, cited by Derrida, p. 967, 54). This is the formal, legal-philosophical version of the figure of thought that Blanchot describes as the "innocence inside evil".

Justice is the domain in which a decision is necessary because the formal application of the law is not sufficient. Justice consists in a decision; and the decision is performed within the field of justice. Since a decision has always to be made in a concrete individual case, which cannot be dealt with in its particularity by the general application of the law, any morally demanding decision takes place above an abyss of undecidability. The decision has to be made in the concrete and particular case, and yet it has to be universal, in accord with the universal. The decision is precisely the accomplishment of this articulation of the singular and the universal; it has to be just to the individual, without being unjust with regard to the universal. It is directed at the "singularity of the other" (955, 41); this singularity is the criterion in any particular case and at the same time, it is in accord with the universal of justice: a universal justice at all times, for every individual.

Justice is essentially related to the other. It concerns, as Thomas Aquinas writes, *ac-*

tiones quae sunt ad alterum (s.th. II. ii 58, 3). Emmanuel Levinas forced the conceptual figure of alterity. A strong concept of the other cannot be thought on the basis of the universal concept of humanity, which would be to occlude its situation of alterity in that which is common to every human being. The concept of the other demands rather that the universal of humanity be thought starting out from the other, as the individual in any given case. If justice has its criterion in the other, then it cannot be a pre-given idea; it has to begin with the other, and to be modified by the singularity of the other (p. 965, 52). The just decision is located in the tension between the singular and the universal, and it is only as a singular and occasional universal that it is just; hence its essence is undecidability. It takes place in a field that is fundamentally marked by non-knowledge – not something that one contingently does not know in a given situation, but an essential non-knowledge. Since the decision has nonetheless to be taken here and now, since "justice does not wait" (p. 967, 53), in a strict and formal sense, it has the structure of madness, if this latter can be understood as absence of knowledge and insight.

4 Anomy

Does my story seem banal?
You've put your finger on it:
it's banality itself.
Blanchot: *The Most High* (p. 87)

Max Aue, the protagonist of Littell's *The Kindly Ones*, born in 1913, is another Oresteian figure.[39] The fact of being fatherless is the decisive element of his psychic constitution. His father, like Agamemnon, is absent during the war, and in the period following it, and disappears definitively when the boy is 8 years old. The mother does not kill him, but lets him be declared dead, in order to be able to marry the Frenchman, Moreau. The son "never really loved" his mother, "even hated her" (K, 22, 28); he transfigured the absent father, and compensated for his absence by identifying with Germany, with National Socialism, and with the Führer. With his excellent knowledge of Greek and Greek literature, Aue is aware of his Oresteian complex. In Paris, he frequents right-wing national circles, and the editorial offices of the anti-Semitic journal, *Je suis partout*, put out by Robert Brasillach. Brasillach sees the friendship between Thomas Hauser and Max Aue in terms of the ancient myth. "Is he your Pylades?", Brasillach asked me maliciously in Greek. "Exactly", Thomas retorted in the same language [...] "And he is my Orestes" (K, 57, 60).

From the beginning of the novel, the appeal of the narrator to his "human brothers" places his narrative in a larger context. It is not only the story of Max Aue; his particular story has a general significance that concerns all humans. "And also this concerns you: you'll see that this concerns you". For this reason, this is an "edifying" story, "a real morality play" (K, 3, 11). The story becomes readable as the narration of morality itself. The processes of mechanization, industrialization and also bureaucratization, by which the practice of killing is modernized and rationalized, places a technical and organizational apparatus in between the killer and his act, so that the individual responsible is no longer immediately the one who performs the act of killing. The examples that Aue gives are intended to show that no-one can exculpate himself from acting the same way in a given situation, and from doing what he is told. Studies on the authoritarian character or the Milgram experiment have made this point. This is where the fraternity and the common identity of the "human brothers" lies. They are brothers in the spirit of the authoritarian character. This is why the story of Max Aue is the narration of morality itself: "The ordinary men that make up the State – especially in unstable times – now

[39] Jonathan Littell: *Les bienveillantes*, Paris, Gallimard, 2006 / *The Kindly Ones*, translated by Charlotte Mandell, London, Chatto and Windus, 2009. This novel is cited in parentheses with the abbreviation (K); the first number refers to the English translation, and the second to the original French.

there's the real danger. The real danger for mankind is me, is you" (K, 21, 27-28). Max Aue's story is about the "ordinary men who make up the state". His psychic constitution, the war, and national Socialism have entered into a synthesis which has produced the events of his story. And he shares this constitution with everyone else, since he is a "man like any other, a man like you...I am just like you" (K, 24, 30). Henri Sorge makes the same claim in *The Most High*: "I was anybody. How can you forget that phrase?" (MH, 1, 9) The elements of the myth of Orestes form the deep structure of this modern Everyman. In conversation with Jesús Ruiz Mantilla, Littell said that he wanted to answer "a simple question" with the novel: "What is the nature of state crime?"

The discussion about the extermination of the European Jews in Germany has been carried on for some time now in terms of the testimony of the victim. For this reason, too, Littell's novel, which takes up the perspective (fictive, moreover) of the agent, has been seen as offensive. Susan Rubin Suleiman and Liran Razinski read *The Kindly Ones* in this perspective. In *Eichmann in Jerusalem*, Hannah Arendt showed that the testimony of the victim is inadequate in the trials of war-criminals, since the majority of the victims have not survived; and the actors in the crime are themselves not suitable witnesses. Above all, however, testimony is not the appropriate category in this context since it does not bring out the particularity of the crime. A witness is a particular authority; whether as victim or offender, the witness testifies to a particular crime. What is new about this crime, however, is that it is a mass-murder carried out by a bureaucracy; and the consequence is that there can be no witnesses for the criminals or their crimes. Testimony dissolves into a web of bureaucratic files and records. The particular witness remains on the level of the particular murder, and does not attain the global dimension of the genocide. Genocide is not a crime against many individuals, but a crime against humanity. Therefore, what is necessary is first to develop an adequate conception of such a crime. Such a conception would have to be founded in the recognition that this crime destroys the unity of humanity and the "essence of the human race", that it destroys humanity as the common property of peoples. Genocide is an act of enmity against mankind. Eichmann is the agent of this enmity and therefore an enemy of mankind.

The uncanny element of this structure is that the individual, as the representative and the agent of this enmity, can only act because his actions are carried by the powerful administrative apparatus. The hostile act has at once a particular and a universal dimension. On the level of the particular, the actions of any given individual, taken in themselves, do not appear as criminal, and so they cannot be testified to as crimes by eyewitnesses. Filling out forms and processing files is not a crime. Nonetheless, taken together, on the general level of the administration as a mechanism, all of these particular acts produce the crime of genocide. Hannah Arendt does not simply say that this collaboration of the individual and the general as a condition for the genocide is banal: she speaks rather of the banality of evil. One should see this term as an attempt to theoretically articulate what is new in the crime of genocide. Evil is the traditional general category, and banality here marks the specific difference. The banality of this modern evil consists in the cooperative effect of banal individual acts carried out within the framework of a total administrative apparatus. It is the apparatus that gives the banality its uncanny dimension. To understand it is the theoretical task of the time.

Littell recognized this problem of the impossibility of testimony with respect to the most essential aspect of the genocide, and found a solution. The novel deals with the extermination of the Jews from the point of view of the criminals; in the strict sense, they are the only possible witnesses. If the aim of the campaign was the extermination of the Jewish people, then the perpetrator remains as the sole witness. The problem of the interdependence of the individual and the apparatus is articulated by Max Aue, who does indeed have individual traits, but who is finally conceived as a type. He is the allegorical figure of the crime that becomes genocide by virtue of the interaction of the individual and the administrative mechanism. This "inter-action" is the model of enmity against mankind. The divergence between criminal and crime is not a split within a particular person, such as Adolf Eichmann or Max Aue, who could be understood by a character analysis. It is precisely for this reason that Littell gives a mythical structure to the general constitution of the character.

Immediately after characterizing Max Aue's history as an edifying narrative, there follows an image of the transformation of a caterpillar into a butterfly. This passage inscribes the work in the tradition of the autobiographical account of inner experience, leading to the metamorphosis of a conversion. The head-wound in Stalingrad and its consequences are later explicitly conceived by Aue as the agent of such a metamorphosis, from the old to the new Adam (K, 432, 400). Certainly, at the beginning of the novel the image of the metamorphosis is only introduced *ex negativo*. One waits in vain for the transformation into the "butterfly that we bear in ourselves [...], the nymph stage never comes, we remain larvae" (K, 3, 11). Towards the end of the novel another image of metamorphosis is evoked. While crossing a river, Aue, like Narcissus, wants to contemplate his reflected image, and then falls into the water, from which he is saved by his companion (K, 848, 925). But again, the metamorphosis evoked by the myth does not transpire – unless writing is finally the right form of metamorphosis for Aue, and his report is his "butterfly" or his "flower".

The first chapter introduces a sequence of motives which unfold in the narrative that follows. The constellation of these motifs reveals the meaning of the story. This concerns, on the one hand, the domain of politics and law, right and justification. Aue is convinced that he "has nothing to justify [...] I do not regret anything: I did my work, that's all" (K, 4-5, 11). He has a doctorate in law, and has the literary and philosophical knowledge in order to be able to reflect upon his own actions at a theoretically advanced level. After receiving his doctorate in 1939, he has a conversation with his superior in his first posting with the security service on the relation between the individual and the state. In a dialectical figure reminiscent of Hegel, the individual is conceived as the negation of the state; war, then, is the negation of the negation, forming the people into a genuine unity (K, 54-55, 58). Correspondingly, in the conceptual center of the novel, Aue proposes a theory of the categorical imperative under the conditions of the National Socialist Führer-principle and the legal force of the Führer's command (K, 101-102,100-101; 567, 522).

On the other hand, the meaning of the tale concerns the domain of the body and of the elementary vital functions: "I have remained someone who believes that the only things indispensable to human life are air, food, drink, and excretion, and the search for truth. The rest is optional" (K, 5, 12). The constellation of vital functions and the search for truth, of body and truth, needs to be understood conceptually. The truth in question is that of the special form of the political, created by National Socialism, and by fascism more generally, of which Max Aue is the emblematic incarnation; it is grounded in a particular psycho-physical constitution, the particular configuration of the oral and the anal, which forms the dispositive of his personality, and whose clearest forms of expression are diarrhea and vomiting. On the level of the affects, there is a corresponding anxiety, which Aue traces back to his childhood (K, 6, 13-14), and an equally elementary feeling of disgust.

Both syndromes become acute in response to acts of war. The first attacks of vomiting and diarrhea occur after a mass-execution in the Ukraine. They are the immediate physical expression of the feeling that is expressed in German as in French: *chier de peur, Schiss haben, c'est dégueulasse – das ist zum Kotzen*, to shit oneself, in English. The shitting is ambivalently over-determined, caused by both the death-anxiety of the victim, and the guilt-anxiety of the executioner. It is the ambivalence motif at the deepest physical level – the symbol of the Germans, for whom *die Scheiße* (shit) is the essential profanity.

The vomiting attacks are prefigured in Aue's childhood. A childhood memory links it to the father and to the fear of his authority, his rage and his punishment (K, 881, 807). For Max Aue, there is a direct relation between the corporeal and the symbolic levels. Hence the absolute interruption of the symbolic order, the ultimate transgression of incest, is prefaced with an attack of vomiting. After having mentioned that he was at first sea-sick on the boat-trip with his stepfather, he describes the beginning of his incestuous relationship with his sister. And in one of his hallucinatory fantasies during his stay at the estate of Üxküll, he connects his anal-faecal obsession with incest. He fantasizes a fusion with his twin sister as an absolute independence, free of alterity, a narcissistic self-sufficiency, that extends to the elementary physical level in "startling fantasies" and "the demented vision of perfect coprophagic autarchy." "This way, we were self-sufficient, without loss and without trace, neatly." This "aberrant vision", at the same time, fills him with a "sordid anguish" (K, 886, 812). This vision corresponds on the political level to the phantasms of racial purity and to the taboo against miscegenation. The incest taboo, as the imperative of exogamy and alterity, is the foundation of every civilization; it commands the opening on to the outside and the other.

Between these two poles – the symbolic and the law, as well as that of the physical and of incest – lies the complex of the affective and the mental, the drive-structure and Aue's "family-romance". In his note on the "family romance" of the neurotic, Freud underlined the "liberation of an individual, as he grows up, from the authority of his parents" as the decisive agonistic material of this romance. Its solution, he argues, is necessary for the health of the individual and the "progress of society."[40] The various forms taken by the family romance give rise to the various types of personality and illness. In Aue's case, the family romance is constructed from structural elements belonging to the psychotic. It is grounded as well in the particular relations Max Aue has to his parents. The extremely high valuation of the absent father, the profound hatred of the mother and the stepfather, whom (all indices suggest) he kills, are prefigured in the myth of Orestes. From Aeschylus to Blanchot's *The Most High*, the close sibling love of Electra and Orestes is a fundamental moment of the Oresteian structure. The incestuous

[40] Sigmund Freud: *Family Romances*, in: Sigmund Freud: *The Standard Edition of the Complete Psychological Works of Sigmund Freud, Vol IX (1906-1908) Jensen's Gradiva and other works*, p. 235.

love between the non-identical twins gives their relationship an additional affective intensity. Aue's manifest homosexuality, which he adopts as a substitute after the end of the relationship to his sister, is prefigured in the friendship between Orestes and Pylades. This complex of sibling incest and male homosexuality forms the obverse face of the relationship between Aue and his parents.

Aue himself tries to understand his inner-life and his personal history through the figure of the substitute. He studies law as a substitute for studying literature and philosophy; listening to music serves him as a substitute for playing music; his relationships with men are a substitute for his relationship with his sister, and even more, for his wish to be a woman. The incestuous relationship with his sister begins after the definitive disappearance of his father, and is in an intricate way a substitute for the father. The loss of the father is the original loss. On the other hand, the fascist state and above all, the Führer himself, is a substitute for the father. In fantasies which border on madness, he identifies the Führer with the father, who "might even, if such had been his fate, who knows, have been there in his place" (K, 465, 430). Ultimately, the factory and the director's post that he occupies, belong in this series of substitute formations. He substantiates his special aptitude for administering a large organization that he "did in fact have quite a bit of experience in this area" (K, 11, 18): his organizational activity in the camps, above all, in Auschwitz. A particular correspondence shows how, even in the smallest details, Aue's trajectory is based in his family romance. The factory that he works for makes lace (K, 23, 29); and he notes the "nightgown with the lace collar" on the body of his murdered mother (K, 530, 489).

The core of the economy of drives animating this substitute world is the wish to be a woman. It has a double origin. On the one hand, it stems from envy of female sexuality which, for Aue, is the summit of human possibilities of pleasure and experience. He refers to the prostrate, stimulated in anal penetration, as the "clitoris of the poor man"; and he says that "the prostrate and war are God's two gifts to man to compensate him for not being a woman" (K, 200, 189). He refers to the hole that is opened in his head after being shot in Stalingrad as his third eye, but also as this "gaping vagina in the middle of my forehead" (K, 514, 474). On the other hand, the desire to be a woman is the substitute for his impossible love for his sister, the only woman he loved "more than everything in the world". His homosexuality is the expression of this wish for feminization. "It is quite conceivable that by dreaming of myself as a woman, by dreaming of myself in a woman's body, I was still seeking her, I wanted to draw closer to her, I wanted to be like her, I wanted to be her" (K, 23, 29). He looks at men "with the eyes of a woman", in the knowledge that they are "put there for the pleasure of women" (K, 165, 158).

His desire to be a woman peaks in the fantasy of the female orgasm as an experience dissolving the limits. He wants to be a woman "naked, on her back, her legs spread wide open, crushed beneath the weight of man, clinging to him and pierced by him, drowning in him as she becomes the limitless sea in which he himself is drowned, a pleasure that's endless and beginningless too" (K, 23, 29). The pleasure in anal penetration corresponds to this desire, which ever again gives him the same experience of dissolution. "For him, my ass opened like a flower, and when he finally slipped it in, a ball of white light began to grow at the base of my spine, slowly rose up my back and annihilated my head" (K, 501, 462). The fantasy of feminization is an elementary component in Aue's drive-structure. It is a substitute for the relationship to the sister, which for its part, substitutes for the lost father, and the symbolic order that he represents. This order is replaced by the order of the party and of National Socialism. After a similar experience of dissolution – triggered by the marriage of his sister in 1938, one can presume – he enters into the security service, "his ass full of sperm". Robert Brasillach translates this fantasy of feminization into the political plane, transposing it to the occupation of France – La France – by the Germans. "We have slept with Germany, and the memory will remain sweet to us" (K, 510, 470).[41]

Aue's wish to be a woman corresponds to basic elements of the system of madness described by Daniel Paul Schreber in his autobiographical report, *Memoirs of my Nervous Illness* (1903). Psychoanalysts from Freud to Lacan and beyond have recognized elementary traits of the constitution of psychosis in Schreber's *Memoirs*.[42] The "cultivation of femininity" is part of Schreber's psychosis (p. 164). It begins with "the idea that it really must be rather pleasant to be a woman succumbing to intercourse" (p. 46). The idea then develops into a fantasy of castration, in which, "the [external] male genitals [...] are retracted into the body", and then "the inner sex organs are transformed into the corresponding female organs" (p. 60). Emasculation is part of the divine plan for a new organization of "the world order". This experience includes an infinite intensification of "soul-voluptuousness", which gives Schreber "the impression of a female body" (p. 163), and a "pretty definite foretaste of female sexual enjoyment during intercourse" (p. 289). This transformation is "in accordance with the essence of the Order of the World" (p. 255); its purpose is "the creation of new human beings" (p. 121), and "the renewal of mankind" (p. 255).

The parallels between Aue and Schreber, however, make it clear that Aue does not develop a psychosis, even if he recurrently slips into altered states of consciousness. But it may be that, in place of the system of madness and the psychotic "influence-apparatus" (Victor Tausk) – a pathological version of what Freud calls the "psychic apparatus" – the political system steps in, that is to say, National Socialism and the fascist state-apparatus, which, in the second part of the novel, becomes the apparatus of annihilation. After the death of his father, his orientation towards the Führer and his politics shields him against an outbreak of manifest psychosis. This could mean, however, that this politics represents a form of collective psychosis. The Oresteian myth would then provide the deep structure of the psychotic political formation, and Max Aue would be its emblematic type. The principle of state-formation – that is to say, the movement by which the individual becomes a citizen, the transformation of the individual will into the general will, the transition from the individual to the state – is mediated by the family. The identification of the father with the Führer is the specific factor that makes Max Aue into a citizen. In Aue, as in Henri Sorge, the condition of the modern Everyman, living in an equally normal community, is recognizable; but each of the novels distorts this normality into transparency. In Henri Sorge, we see the psychotic

41 Sartre took up this motif in *The Flies*. The city of Argos is *une femme en rue*. He comments on this in his essay on the collaborator.

42 Daniel Paul Schreber: *Memoirs of my Nervous Illness*, translated by Ida Macalpine and Richard Hunter, Harvard College, 1955. Reprinted by New York Review of Books, 2000. References with page-number in parenthesis.

ground, the paranoid deep structure of the norm – and in Max Aue, its political consequences.

The correspondence between the personal history of Aue and the political history of Germany forms the structural principle of *The Kindly Ones.* The "passionate desire for the absolute and for transgression", born out of the particular situation of the childhood of Aue, finds its fulfilment in the politics of National Socialism. "I had always wanted my thinking to be radical; and now the State, the nation had also chosen the radical and the absolute; how, then, just at that moment, could I turn my back, say no, and at the end of the day, prefer the comfort of bourgeois laws, the mediocre assurance of the social contract" (K, 96, 95). To the extent that Aue is a modern Everyman and his make-up that of social normality, the opposition between radical politics and the "bourgeois laws" of the "social contract" appears as superficial, concealing a deeper identity.

The childhood memories that come back to Aue in the extreme situations of the war are an aspect of this correspondence. The bungled execution of a boy makes him remember the games of his own childhood, which become ever more bizarre after the disappearance of his father. Self-strangulation gives him a sensation of dissolving, which he experiences as "keen pleasure and boundless freedom" (K, 108, 110). At the executions he experiences the "insurmountable feeling of a transgression, of a monstrous violation of the Good and the Beautiful"; they give him "the sensation of a rupture, an infinite disturbance of my whole being" (K, 179, 170). The blood and the faeces of the victims in the mass grave, through which he wades amidst the sprawl of bodies, remind him of the diarrhea that he had experienced as a child on vacation in Spain, and that returns after the executions. The swarm of cockroaches on the Spanish toilets and the writhing of the bodies in the mass-grave are both affective images for the dissolving core of his personality. Along the same lines, as he is about to give an already wounded girl the mercy shot, he fantasizes that his arm comes loose from his body and shoots by itself (K, 130, 125/26).

Such a fantasy is less an attempt to distance himself from his acts than a symptom of dissociation. During the execution of a young woman, who he finds "unspeakably beautiful", and who he idealizes as Notre-Dame-des-Neiges – Our Lady of the Snow – he has a fantasy of total dissolution. "She looked at me, a clear luminous look, washed of everything, and I saw that she understood everything, knew everything, and faced with this pure knowledge I burst into flames. My clothes cracked, the skin of my belly melted, the fat sizzled, fire roared in my eye sockets and my mouth, and cleaned out the inside of my skull. The blaze was so intense she had to turn her head away. I burned to a cinder, my remains were transformed into a salt statue; soon as it cooled down, pieces broke off, first a shoulder, then a hand, then half the head. Finally I finished collapsing at her feet and the wind swept away the pile of salt and scattered it" (K, 179, 171). His anal penetration by his male lover has a similar effect; he describes it as being "like a blue, luminous stream of molten lead filling your pelvis and rising slowly up your spine to seize your head and erase it" (K, 200, 189). Since his first homosexual experience in the boarding school, he seeks in it "the oceanic pleasure of a woman" (K, 203, 192) and the "boundless pleasure" of incest with his sister (K, 201, 190).

When Aue, at the end of the war, visits his sister and takes up the strangulation-play again, *Notre-Dame des Neiges* – Our Lady of the Snow – appears in the interstitial zone between reality and fantasy; and again, it is as an expression of the increasing dissociation of personality and the general dissolution of political structures in Germany (K, 912, 834-835). This dissociation is the basis of the personality-structure and the state-structure which are set up to contain it. The "radical desire for the absolute and for transgression", which leads him to the "edge of mass-graves in the Ukraine", stems from the personality-dissociation which originated with the loss of the father. The disappearance of the father, the set of wishes and desires that originates with this disappearance, and their fulfilment in the politics of National Socialism, form one complex.

The hatred of the mother corresponds to the loss of the father. But it also has deeper origins. When a wounded man in Stalingrad calls out for his mother, it sets off an episode of recollection in Aue. He hates his mother since she had his father declared dead and married his stepfather Moreau. This hatred continues into the present. But he suspects that there may be a beloved mother behind the one he hates, one for whom, in an emergency, he, too, would call out. The relation to the mother is deeply ambivalent. As an infant, he had a "dangerous allergy against his mother's milk"; but as a child he had swooned in the odour of her body with "senseless delight"; it was like a "return into the lost womb". The deepest reason for his hatred of his mother is that she had given birth to him: "that insanely arrogant right she had granted herself to bring me into the world" (K, 370, 343). For him, this means that she drove him out of the paradise of the uterus. Aue's predilection for hot baths originates with this syndrome; "it was soft and gentle like amniotic fluid, I stayed in as long as possible" (K, 706, 649). The sweating cure that he takes to cure his fever after the definitive collapse of his father image leads him also to a uterine regression-fantasy, which is the obverse side of the hatred of the mother. The bedding is "warm and reassuring like a uterus from which I never wanted to emerge, a dark, silent elastic paradise, agitated only by the rhythm of my heartbeats and my blood flowing, an immense organic symphony […] I bathed in my sweat as in amniotic fluid, I would have liked my birth not to exist" (K, 811, 745).

The deepest depths of Aue's drive-structure, the configuration of his affects and his relation to the world, lie in this relation to the mother. The refused breast is its mythical image. When the memory of this family-romance comes over him – "violently" (K, 369, 342) – in Stalingrad, it is suggested that the deep structure of the war lies in this archaic, wild, uncontrolled hatred of the infant towards the mother's breast, the mythical "bad breast". This hatred becomes manifest through the loss of the father, and the betrayal of the mother. "It had always existed, it came from elsewhere, from a world that was not the world of men and of everyday work, a world that was usually sealed but whose doors the war could suddenly throw open, freeing in a hoarse, inarticulate brutal shout its gaping darkness, a pestilential swamp, overturning the established order of things, customs and laws, forcing men to kill each other, putting them back under the yoke from which they had with so much difficulty liberated themselves, the weight of all that came before" (K, 373, 346).

The end of the novel corresponds to this complex. It is a sequence of subterranean spaces, all of which are dark, wet and cold. An "underground tunnel" leads into the Führer's bunker, where he is given a decoration, and then bites or pinches the Führer on the nose. The bunker-space is itself under water, and an "abominable stench of urine filled the bunker, mixed with the misty effluvia of mildew, sweat and wet wool" (K, 958, 878-879). The prison into which he is then thrown is a "concrete room, bare and wet". "Puddles dotted the ground; the walls were sweating; and the lock on the door plunged me into an absolute uterine darkness" (K, 961, 881). And the subway shaft into which he flees is once again a "descent into the darkness"; the walls and the ceiling are dripping with moisture, and the tracks stand under water (K, 884, 964). The fantasy of a regression into the uterus is given an uncanny reality.

It is possible that all of these underground shelters and passage-ways, which Aue integrates into his fantasies, are themselves fantasies that have been built into the real world. The Führer's bunker, then, signifies that the Führer is himself such stuff as Aue is made on. It is for this reason that, at the moment at which he sees the truth of his father and the mirror of himself in him – a small, pathetic man with bad breath – he can only respond with a displacement activity which is also a symbolic castration. The gap between the phantasmatic image of the Führer and his reality as a person – corresponding to that between the father-imago and the actual father of Aue – causes the whole system to collapse for Aue.

In this way, we can understand why he is confronted with his family-romance, immediately after this scene. The policemen Weser and Clemens, who are pursuing him for the murder of his mother and his stepfather, suddenly re-appear, as they had earlier on the estate of Üxküll. In the code of a realistic action, this would be improbable, but in the code of the psychic constitution of Aue, it is necessary. The policemen appear as a hallucinatory projection on the part of Aue; he has integrated real-world policemen into the cast of his own family-romance as figures of his guilt. They emerge from out of this romance to figure in his real experience, and in the space between reality and madness, are able to act in the manner of phantasms in the real world. The policemen, as figures of an incipient madness, show that madness is a form of right and law which has become disfunctional, and that the constitution of the law is a contained kind of madness.

The police confront Aue with details about the murder, which coincide with his memories, and possibly originate from them. Aue counters the suggestion that his mother may have shown him her breast before her death, as Clytemnestra did to Orestes, in order to remind him that she is his mother – "Have pity child, upon this breast" (*Libation-Bearers*, v. 896) – with his allergic reaction against the (poisoned) milk of his mother. The "bad breast" as the figure of the love-hate relationship between mother and son is the *dispositif* of an idolizing construction of the father-figure and the symbolic order and the law that develops with it.

At the end of the novel, Weser and Clemens preface their reconstructed account of the murder of his mother with the same formula with which the book had begun: "We're going to tell you how it happened" (K, 966, 886). Aue himself begins his report by saying: "Oh my human brothers, let me tell you how it happened" (K, 4, 11). The correspondence makes it clear that the mythical sub-text, the deep structure of the story, makes up its content. With his report, Aue replies to Leopold von Ranke's historical dictum from the preface to the *History of the Latin and Germanic Nations* that the task of history is not to "to judge the past, or to instruct the present for the benefit of future ages" but only "to show what actually happened" (*wie es eigentlich gewesen*). He gives the historiographical report a mythical dimension that shows the truth-content of the events. In conversation with Samuel Blumenfeld, Littell identified the improbability of the character Aue as the particular quality of his novel: "It was not a matter of probability, for me", he remarked, "but of truth. You cannot create a novel if you insist solely on plausibility. Novelistic truth is a different thing from historic or sociological truth." The probable draws its meaning from the way things actually were, from reference. The "truth of a novel" is not referential but figurative. Against the background of the historiographic account, the novel takes on its particular profile. The story is indeed "edifying" (K, 3, 11), but not in a judgmental or didactic sense, rather in the analytical sense of the French moralist tradition, when they describe the affective structures and the patterns of conduct that derive from them.

Aue's incestuous relationship with his sister begins after his mother's remarriage and the emergence of his open hatred for her, and compensates for the loss of the father-figure. This is why, in an "unhoped for return" in Stalingrad, he recollects the peak of the sibling love. "It was the age of pure innocence, superb, magnificent. Freedom possessed our narrow little bodies [...] we rolled, twisted together in the dust, our naked bodies indissociable, neither one nor the other specifically girl or boy, but a couple of snakes intertwined" (K, 405, 375). Aue himself recognized the paradigm of this family-structure in the myth of the Atrides. During his time at the boarding school (to which he is sent after the discovery of the incest), he takes the part of Electra in a staging of his favorite play, Sophocles' *Electra*, identifying thereby with his sister. In Stalingrad he finds by chance a copy of the play, and the correspondence between the events of the war and the childhood memory becomes apparent. He was "possessed with hatred and love and the sensation of my young virgin's body" and became both Electra and Orestes, combined in one. The affective core of the Oresteian complex in Max Aue is the introduction of the sibling-incest into the mythic paradigm; this synthesis dictates the disastrous relationship with the parents and the "happy and paradisiacal" period of incest that makes up for the loss of the parents: "the butchery in the House of Atreus was the blood in my own house" (K, 411, 380-381).

The long fever-fantasy after the head-wound sustained in Stalingrad and the period of convalescence that follows mark a caesura in the life of Max Aue. The literal midpoint of the book is occupied by the meeting of Max Aue and his sister in Berlin (K, 442-459). The passages which describe the head-wound and its immediate consequences and those that recount the murder of his mother and stepfather are approximately equidistant from this center. The correspondence between the two has its point of articulation in the relationship to the sister. As he recalls his incestuous relationship with his sister, before the murder, it reminds him at once of the fever-fantasy after his injury. "I dove into these sensations as I had plunged into the Volga, with complete abandon" (K, 523, 482). The head-wound at first causes a complete dissociation of mind and body. Aue is "completely detached from his body" and "really scattered" (K, 431, 399). A "new Adam" (K, 432, 400), he has to reassemble himself and the world. At first, however, in looking in the mirror, the result is a "mosaic of diverse features", "a collection of pieces that fit together well enough, but that came from different puzzles" (K, 435, 403). The evocation of the topos of the "new Adam" gives the passage the status of the turning point, the conversion that forms the center of the traditional spiritual autobiography. "Nothing will ever be the same again" (K, 404, 436). The convalescence that follows takes place in the Berlin Hotel Eden. The location links this central sequence with the "happy and paradisiacal" incest, but also with the fantasy of the maternal uterus as paradise.

The physical correlate of the conversion is the hole, created by the bullet-wound to his head. It has healed over, but now becomes an absurd center of his personality. He asks himself if *un trou puisse aussi être un tout* (K, 436, 404). The question now is that of this minimal difference between *trou* (hole) and *tout* (whole): the hole as empty and as a whole – *le trou et le tout* – whereby the whole develops itself out of the emptiness and as emptiness – *le trou est le tout et le tout et le trou*. "My thinking about the world now had to reorganize itself around this world" (K, 436, 404). The hole is the basic figure for the psychic state of Aue and, by extension, for that of National Socialist Germany: it corresponds to the annihilation of the 6th Army in Stalingrad.

The fact that Aue imagines the hole in his head as "a third eye, a pineal eye" (K, 443, 410) once again fits into the framework of the spiritual autobiography and the report of the inner experience. The transformation is not illuminating, but darkening; the third eye is "directed towards darkness, gifted with the power of looking at the bare face of death, and of grasping this face behind each face [...] beneath the smiles, through the palest, healthiest skin, the most laughing eyes." (K, 443, 410). The transformation has the character of a catastrophe, of the disaster as total ruin.[43] Aue associates it with the entry into the world, with birth, which he conceives as banishment from paradise and a ban on returning, and also with his separation from his sister. The nine months in the uterus are the only period of rest; birth is a banishment into hell (K, 443, 410); the separation is "pure, deadly terror" (K, 448, 414). The loss of the original unity with the mother with birth, the loss of the feeling of union in the incestuous relationship with his sister, Una, after his separation from her, and the loss of physical cohesion and of the relation to the world after the bullet-wound form one complex, whose affective mode is "pure deadly terror" of the disaster and whose figure is the hole in the head and in his personality.[44] The Oresteian narrative provides its mytho-psychic configuration. Since the father is absent, since the father-function is lacking, loss and frustration are not symbolically contained, and take instead the form of a wild hatred for the mother.

In place of the absent father, a series of substitute figures enter into the picture, in general associated with politics, in particular, with the political system of National Socialism. Dr Mandelbrod is super-father. He knew and liked Aue's father and grandfather, and took care of the family after the father's death. He helped Aue in his career, and forms a link between Aue's father and National Socialism; he not only has access to the highest-ranking members of the Party, but even seems to outrank them and to influence them in certain ways. He is a partly mythic, partly fantastic, partly realistic fig-

[43] "The disaster was already there and they didn't realize it, since the disaster is the very idea of the disaster to come, which ruins everything long before term" (K 443, 410). The sentence is an echo of the beginning of Blanchot's *The Writing of the Disaster*. Here the correspondence to Blanchot and his work, which is carried on throughout the novel, is intensified to the point at which it becomes uncanny. See Maurice Blanchot: *L'écriture du désastre*, Paris, Gallimard, 1980 / *The Writing of the Desaster*, translated by Ann Smock. Lincoln: University of Nebraska Press, 1986.

[44] When Aue refers to the hole in his head as "this gaping vagina in the middle of my forehead" (K, 514, 474), this evidently corresponds to the complex of fantasies concerning the nothingness of the female sex organ, which is at the same time infinitely more than the male organ (K, 895-908, 820-832).
The nothingness, the emptiness and the hole in the head form a complex which has its poetological vanishing point in the closing citation from Guillem IX of Aquitaine: "I'll make a song about nothing at all" (K, 913, 836).

ure.[45] He belongs to the leading circles of German industry, and he seems to have been already active in its "founding years". He is strangely ageless, even ancient, a fantastically powerful, string-pulling puppet-master figure, for whom the National Socialists are only pawns in a greater plan, which never becomes clear in the novel. If the aim were the maximization of profits for industry, he would not need to defect to the Soviet Union at the end. He vaguely refers to "more important values" than "the beloved fatherland – *la mère patrie*". The formula is a key for the psychic state of Aue and of National Socialist Germany; it points to the particular constellation of father and mother as the deep structure of a certain form of the political. The Führer, who represented this order, was obviously helpful to Mandelbrod. "But the ontological war, which he has begun, is not finished yet. Who except for Stalin could complete the work?" The ontological war here is a reference to the *gigantomachia* for being and its relation to appearance, in Plato's *Sophist*. The National Socialists would be an agent in the project of creating a gigantic world of delusional appearance, which will then be continued on other levels, first in Moscow. "Afterward, we'll see" (K, 971, 890).[46] The state of total delusion corresponds to a total conspiracy, given that it is deliberately created by an international political program. The stinking intestinal gas that Mandelbrod constantly excretes is a variation on the sulphuric-diabolical – and as it were the pneumatic and spiritualized version of Aue's diarrhea. Mandelbrot then is a figure of the devil, who, for the Christian reading, is the agent of delusion, offering the mere appearance of the good in place of the true good (2 Corinthians 11, 14).[47] After the loss of his father and his Führer, Aue is left at the end with only this phantasmatic Super-Führer figure. With his cats, Mandelbrod is reminiscent of Blofeld, the arch-villain of the James Bond films. In the mythic register, with his three female attendants, he is also a kind of mythical super-father figure, even a figure of Fate, the Moira or the Norn above the apparatus of the gods of the National Socialist nomenklatura; the villain as a figure of fate, evil as fate.

In Mandelbrod's ideas on Germany and on the Germans as a chosen people, one can discern a figure of thought that deeply marks the novel. He recognizes that this idea is Jewish in its origins. He even traces the thought of National Socialism back to Moses Hess, and his book, *Rome and Jerusalem*. In his very name, which is explicitly said to "sound Jewish", although he is actually "a pure German of old Prussian stock" (K, 448, 414-415), he is a figure who incarnates the ambivalence of German and Jew, their twin-like character. When Aue imagines the wife of Rudolph Hess wearing the silk underwear of a Jewish girl, this is the farcical aspect of this ambivalence (K, 577, 627-628). This ambivalence is also the reason why he demands that Aue participate in the extermination of the Jews. "All of our great ideas come from the Jews, and we must have the lucidity to recognize it: the Land as promise and accomplishment, the notion of the Chosen People, the concept of purity of blood [...] That's why the Jews, of all our ene-

45 He corresponds to what is named as *They* in Pynchon's *Gravity's Rainbow*.

46 A continuation of the novel is then supposed to narrate the history of communism until its downfall and find a corresponding mythic deep structure for its truth.

47 Jonas Grethlein: *Littells Orestie. Mythos, Macht und Moral in* Les Bienveillantes, Freiburg, Rombach, 2009, has located the "Mephistophelian traits" of Mandelbrod in a layer of the novel which has its origins in the Faust-theme (p. 56).

mies, are the worst, the most dangerous; the only ones who truly deserve being hated. They are our only real competitors in fact" (K, 420-421, 455).

The extermination of the Jews is therefore the urgent political task; and it concerns above all the domain that lies in between the "historical and fateful decision" of the Führer and its practical application. This interval is the space of the political; practical politics consists in acting in accordance with the exigencies of this domain, and in the destruction of the Jews. Such is the task that Mandelbrod assigns to Aue (K, 456, 423). In discussion with Eichmann, Aue grounds this moment of the political in legal-philosophical terms, beginning with the maxim that the Führer's word has legal force. Dr Mandelbrod and his adjutant Herr Leland are the figures of the execution of the Führer's order, of the realization of the will in deeds. The Führer is the figure of will and command, considered as the intellectual capacity for action. The space in between the will and the action has to be assured by a means, an apparatus: the body and its instruments in the case of the individual, the body politic and the state apparatus in the case of the collective. The action is the extermination of the Jews; it makes the space in between will and deed into the empty space vacated by the Jews who have been exterminated. The content of this conception of the political is the extermination of the enemy. If the enemy is "our own question, posed as a figure" (Theodore Däubler), then the destruction of the enemy is the hole in the body politic, the gap in the polity.

Max Aue's reactions to Hitler's speech of the 21st March, 1943 unfold this ambivalence still more clearly, linking it to his own family-romance. The speech reminds him of the first speech of Hitler that he heard in Munich, during a trip to Germany after his final school examinations. At the time, he had seen similarities between the Führer and his father, and in a phantasmatic hyperbole, identified the two, even fantasized the father in the place of the Führer. "He was saying, as I knew with absolute certainty, the things that my father would have said, if he had been present; if he had still been there, he would have certainly been on the platform; one of the men close to that man, one of his foremost companions; he might even, if such had been his fate, who knows have been there in his place. What's more, the Führer looked like him, when he stood still" (K, 465-466, 430). This identification is nothing but wishful fantasy. His mother had destroyed all the photographs of his father, so he has only vague childhood memories on which to build this imagining. He does not even recognize his father in a photograph that Mandelbrod gives to him. The wish-fantasy is a key to the link between the family-romance and the political; a direct path leads from the loss of the father to the German people and to the Führer. The loss of the father is compensated by the Führer and the National Socialist state, whose politics consists in war and the destruction of the Jews. The constellation of loss and compensatory substitution through war and destruction makes up the core of the psychic constitution of Aue.

Another fantastic idea comes over him during the second speech. He sees the Führer as a Jew, with a rabbi's shawl, *tefillin* and side curls. This hallucinatory fantasy is reproduced when he watches the speech on the newsreel at the cinema, and he considers the possibility that, with his third eye, he is able to see through "the opacity of things" (K, 470, 434). Just before this vision, Mandelbrot had shown him the deep affinity between the Germans and the Jews, and explained their enmity as a result of this affinity. As with Jacob and Esau, there can only be the one chosen one; the relationship between Germans and Jews is a family conflict, the extermination a fratricide. Aristotle located the affect-structure of tragedy in the agonistic feelings that develop between those who are close to one another, especially by blood. This is another motivation for the trace of the tragic in the novel. The Führer himself as a Jew – such is the most extreme figure of this affinity, which is at the same time, an enmity. The figure of thought of "brother Hitler" (Thomas Mann) makes the agonistic core visible and reveals the struggle to annihilate the Jews, both politically and psychically, as a struggle against oneself . In his dreams of Jews, Aue finally becomes one, protected by Himmler (K, 794, 729730). The anti-Semitism of Hitler and of the Germans, like all hatreds, says more in the end about the Germans than about the Jews; "for they naturally hate nothing so much as what is most similar to them". Hence the qualities and dangers continually ascribed to the Jews by the Führer in his speeches are such that he "unwillingly described himself". And this observation concerns not Adolf Hitler, the person, but his function, as a representative of the Germans, someone who, like a lens "captured and concentrated the will of the Volk to bring it into focus always at the right point. Thus, even if in those passages he was speaking about himself, wasn't he speaking about us all?" (K, 692, 636). The enemy as the figure in which one poses one's own question – such is the true structure of the tragic; it allows us to understand the schizoid and paranoid character of the political organization that is shaped by this structure. The ironic-sarcastic echo and the physical basis of this *bellum intestinum* appears with the intestinal disruption of diarrhea from which Max Aue constantly suffers.

In the novel, the father complex is superimposed upon the sister complex. The sister-incest is the other side of the father-syndrome; it steps into the place, into the lack that the father leaves behind, which the stepfather must not make up. The loss of the sister, on the other hand, leads Aue to the Führer, the new father. His sister's marriage in 1938 definitively cements his bond to the Party and the Führer. If the incest-prohibition is the foundation of the symbolic order, then incest signifies its dissolution. This is the psychotic core of Aue. National Socialism is the delusional system which he makes his own, in order to save himself from falling into psychosis: a disastrous attempt at healing himself. His sister, who has studied psychoanalysis, sees Hitler as a psychopath. The pathological make-up of Aue, of Hitler, of the Party and of the National Socialist political system mirror each other.

Loss and absence are the moments of the psychic constitution of Aue. His bond to the Führer is a substitute for the lost unity; National Socialism is the a-symbolic form which aims to compensate for the loss. This complex appears as the political-affective core of the novel when his sister demands that he finally grow up and accept loss, separation and absence as realities (486, 449). Max Aue refuses to grow up. He binds himself to the loss, instead of integrating it and transforming it by giving it a symbolic form. National Socialism is not a symbolic form, because it seeks to preserve the phantasm of a pure, integral origin, and makes the desire for destruction of the other into its affective and political center, instead of conceiving the integration of the other as the figure of its own integrity.

Like the *Wandervögel*, with whom he makes contact as soon as he travels to Germany after high school, and like a certain kind of Romantic, Max Aue and those who shared his attitudes are "professional adolescents", who make childhood and youth into a life-style. Romantic yearning (*Sehnsucht*), previously the longing of the troubadours, Minnesänger and Petrarchists provides the psychic *dispositif* that allows one to see the psycho-historical deep structure of this state of mind. While staying on the property of Üxküll, Aue reads the poems of the Troubadours and a version of the Tristan and Isolde story, as well as *L'éducation sentimentale*, the novel in which Flaubert explored the consequences of this *dispositif* under modern conditions (K, 891, 817; 897, 822). The names of Aue's mother and of the twins – Heloïse, Tristan and Orlando (K, 518, 476-477) – allude to this tradition of absolute, passionate love, which in the conception of the novel makes up a field corresponding to the Oresteian motifs. The passionate aspect of love and its charismatic aura originate in the tension and the conflict of ambivalence between love and hate. In relation to the mother this ambivalence can be acted out oedipally, as mother-incest, or following the Oresteian model, as murder of the mother. The Oresteian complex thus appears as a figure of the unresolved conflict of ambivalence.

Aue's visit to his mother and stepfather, and their murder, the climax of the family-romance, marks a new moment in his life. The link between the family-romance and the political dimension becomes apparent during the visit. He discusses German politics with his stepfather, and his disloyalty as a son with his mother. The conversation with the mother brings about an obvious infantilization. "Once again I felt as if I were shrinking; before this imperious voice, these cold eyes, I was going to pieces, I was becoming a fearful child, smaller than the twins. I tried to get control of myself but it was a lost cause" (K, 520, 480). The scene becomes a repetition of the infantile situation, even though it takes place between adults, and with the consciousness of adults. The confrontation with his father's indifference still produces anguish in the son. The mother had the father declared dead in order to give the children access to his bank account, and thus to free them from dependence on the stepfather. What the son took to be a betrayal – and he still takes it thus: "It's as if you killed him" (K, 522, 481) – had in fact been an act of maternal solicitude. The "killing" of the father by the mother had freed up his inheritance for him, allowing him to break with his mother, and take up his life in Germany. "It was his money, you know that very well, and you took it and used it" (K, 481, 522). Hence the particular form that the conflict of ambivalence takes in Aue. The supposed love of the father was actually indifference and inability to love; the supposed hatred of the mother was care and love. The result is a contamination of both the love for the father and the hatred of the mother.

Correspondingly, the memory of the relationship to the sister triggers an "animal terror"; it inspires "a mixture of repulsion and fascination, as if I were holding a live bomb in my hands" (K, 523, 482). Because Aue's incest with his sister is a substitute-formation for the loss of the father, the same ambivalent repulsion and fascination is at work in it. The problematic nexus of the family-romance – laboring "under the weight of the past, of wounds received or imagined, of irreparable mistakes, of the unredeemability of time" (K, 526, 484) – immediately corresponds, in Aue's perception, with the political situation in Germany. This association is prepared by the suspicion that the twins – his own children, conceived during the last incestuous act with his sister in Zürich – could be "little Jews" (K, 525, 484). "In the end, the collective problem of the Germans was the same as my own; they, too, were struggling to extract themselves from a painful past, to wipe the slate clean so they'd be able to begin new things. That was how they arrived at the most radical solution of them all: murder, the painful horror of murder" (K, 525, 485). For Aue, the murder of the Jews and the murder of his mother are two aspects of the same problem. They form a constellation that contains the meaning of the novel's construction: the homology of family and state, the interference of the family-romance and political history.

The confrontation with the bodies of his stepfather and his mother also triggers anguish. His reaction to the corpse of his stepfather – "this contact froze me (*me glaça*)" (530, 488) – corresponds to his reaction to the memory of incest: "the very fact of this past chilled me to the bone (*me glaçait*)" (K, 523, 482). He is "petrified with horror (*pétrifié d'horreur)*" (K, 530, 489), "anguish was suffocating me" (K, 531, 489): "I was petrified with anguish (*pétrifiée d'angoisse*), my thoughts were frozen in place (*figées*)" (K, 531, 490). The affective core of the psychic condition is unremitting fear, triggered, not by the real sight of the corpses, but by their psychic representatives. He is *pétrifiée d'horreur* and *pétrifiée d'angoisse*; the image of petrification refers to the mythical Medusa, the sight of whom turns one to stone.

In a little sketch on "The Medusa's Head", Freud had interpreted the Medusa as a figure for castration. The horror of the Medusa's head expresses the castration-anxiety caused by the sight of the female genitalia; "the multiplication of penis-symbols" – the innumerable snakes that are the hair of the Medusa – "signifies castration". The petrification that results "signifies erection", that is to say, the certainty of not being castrated. Freud interprets the erection as a reaction to the castration-anxiety, which makes it possible and brings it about. The horrifying and pleasurable effects of the female genitals enter into a synthesis in the erection. Hence the essential ambivalence of sexuality. For psychoanalysis, castration is the figure for the interpretation of sexual difference, which triggers anguish – for the man. This anguish is at the same time the condition of possibility of sexuality and of pleasure – which, accordingly, is essentially a pleasure in anxiety.

After the initial loss of the maternal inter-uterine paradise, the loss of the father and then the loss of the sister, Aue also loses his real mother. Since it is not integrated, not transformed into experience and symbolic form, the loss becomes a continual anguish and horror. His first reaction is the desire to return to war, to be transferred to the front. Since he is ineligible for combat-service, he is placed in the administration of the concentration camps, by the mediation of Mandelbrod. His mission is to organize the interned work-force for rational exploitation. Thus Aue and the novel move into the other dimension of National Socialism: the concentration camps and the extermination of the Jews. Aue's participation once again derives from his family-romance. The peripeties of this romance give rise to the desire for direct action, which is then redirected and sublimated into administrative activity. The rational and humane administration of the camp work is a sublimation of his drive and affect fixations. These fixations are not dissolved by the murders, and would otherwise have had to have been acted out in the war. In this sense, the matricide and the final solution form one figurative constellation.[48] The symbolic rise of Aue in the hierarchical order corresponds to this sublimation; he receives

[48] Jonas Grethlein: *Littells Orestie. Mythos, Macht und Moral in* Les Bienveillantes, Freiburg, Rombach, 2009, brings out the "absurdity" of the "transposition" of the genocide of the Jews by the National Socialists on to the matricide of Orestes/Aue (p. 55). On the referential level, such a parallel-action – in which for Aue, in any case, the transposition takes place in the opposite direction – is certainly tendentially revisionist. On the figural level, however, it constructs a metaphor. It articulates the familial constitution of the drives and affects of Max Aue with the political constitution of National Socialism.

the appropriate privileges of office – a chauffeur, an office with a waiting room – , works in Himmler's circles, and has access to the Reichsführer and to the secret documents concerning the final solution. His activity in this position again is configured by the conflict of ambivalence. The final solution demands the extermination of the Jews; the war-industry demands their preservation as a workforce. The state and administrative apparatus is at the same time a machine for destruction, to be rationalized according to criteria of efficiency. Thus the ambivalence is introduced into the extermination of the Jews.

One of the phantasmatic conversations between Aue and his sister on the Uxküll estate concerns the question of guilt. Aue holds to his conviction that the German people had been undermined by its enemies, and that their execution is justified. His twin sister takes the opposing position in this inner disputation; she underlines the ambivalence which, after Mandelbrod's remarks on the grounds of anti-Semitism, took on the form of Aue's hallucinatory vision of Hitler in Jewish costume. In the Jews, the Germans have killed themselves – the inner Jews who are merely the Germans with their German virtues magnified and shown in their true light. For the Jew as seen in anti-Semitism is in fact the German character, which the Jews have imitated and made their own, in order to become assimilated. Anti-Semitism is the self-hatred of the Germans, and as such, an elementary conflict of ambivalence. The story in fact is banality itself. But this banal antagonism seems to make up the structure of right and politics.

The Jew's golden calf is their assimilation of German-ness; in this way, they give up the status of the chosen people. Conversely, the desire of the Germans to be the chosen people is an imitation of the Jews. To be Jewish means to be other. "For if *Jew*, these days, still means anything, it means Other, an Other and an Otherwise that might be impossible, but that are necessary" (K, 875, 802). This means that assimilation is a false step. But the being of the other is characterized by its own ambivalence. The desire and the will to be the chosen people is a phantasmatic and narcissistic fixation, for which the other can only appear as an intruder and an enemy. This collective narcissism appears in the phantasm of purity and in the taboo prohibiting miscegenation: but this is merely the mirror-image of the pure Judaism that wants to remain in the "desert" and refuses to assimilate. Such is the abyss of the conflict of ambivalence. Not to inter-marry and not to assimilate are two moments of the same complex, which takes shape in the phantasm of the chosen people. In this way, the conflict of ambivalence – "many of us would have gladly taken part, but we were not allowed to" (Jacob Taubes) – enters into the deepest levels of the Jewish self-image. What is needed, then, is another conception of otherness, no longer as a category of the self and the same, but rather in relation to the other as the chosen one. The result is a politics of friendship.

Max Aue's dissolution of the conflict of ambivalence is a "strange apathy": this is the affective disposition for his new activity. After reading the letter in which his sister reports the burial of his mother, he perceives a "lack of reaction" in himself, which allows him to immediately return to "work problems". The thought of his sister is "a stove that had gone out and smelled of cold ashes"; the thought of the mother is "a quiet long-neglected gravestone". "This strange apathy extended to all other aspects of my life" (K, 552, 508). Now that it is over, the affective intensity of the perverse family-romance has turned into a complete "lack of reaction". This affective energy is now available to be transformed and channeled into a new activity. At the same time the apathy that comes from the collapse of the family structure is the condition of possibility for the political atrocities. The idea of extermination is administratively realized in an uncanny way with the best will and the best intentions. The uncanny is a transformation of what used to be familiar.

One can see correspondences to the underlying apathy of this conduct at the level of political reality: for example, the concern for a rational, efficient and trouble-free extermination, and the "maximum rational use of available labor" (K, 584, 635): likewise the peculiarly general conventions of language, which serve to designate the brutal reality in an anodine manner: and the passive constructions, which make things happen by themselves, without an agent as in "the Jews have been conveyed to the special treatment"; "in a way they weren't even actions": as a result of a substantivized, verbless speech "there were only facts, brute realities" (K, 631, 581). The conversion of these facts into numbers and statistics on the increasing or decreasing "average rate of mortality" (641, 590) is a further step in the process of abstraction and de-realization. Aue's "enthusiasm" for his work (K, 637, 587) shows that his affective investments have been transferred into his administrative activity. The administrative apparatus provides the structure of his psychic apparatus: the camp becomes a world for him. In his dream of the Great Camp of the World, he imagines "a perfect camp, having reached an impossible point of stasis" (K, 621, 572).

For Aue, it is particularly important to humanize the extermination and to achieve greater productivity through the rationalization of the camp and the improvement of the working conditions. With this idea, he attempts to separate himself subjectively from the ordinary Nazi and to show himself as a true National Socialist, concerned only with the goals of the Party. In this way, the truth of National Socialism becomes recognizable in the conception of the book. If the extermination of the Jews were carried out for its own sake, as an *acte gratuit*, it could be conceived as a figure of radical evil. Given that the extermination is conducted on the basis of racial-political considerations, with the aim of a purification of the German people – Aue gives the highest importance to this point, and since he is well informed theologically and politically, the consequences of the argument are clear to him – it is only logical to draw collateral advantages in labor and profit from the undertaking. The perfidy of this line of argumentation lies in its notion of improvement, which mixes the categories of good and evil in an abyssal way. The better becomes thus a constitutive element of evil, and thus it, too, is shot through with ambivalence. The good of improvement becomes the means of evil; thus the good and the better are corrupted. If the administration of the camps had been more human and efficient, for example, the secret weapon could have been more quickly developed, the war won, and the Germans could have become a respected part of the community of nations (K, 737-744, 678-684). Even during the dismantling of Auschwitz, Aue attempts to institute more humane practices, in order to preserve the utility of the inmates as a workforce (K, 845-858, 775-787).

The character of the Judge, Dr Morgen belongs within the field of this corruption of the good and the right, of justice and law. He is looking into corruption in the camps. For this representative of law and justice, Auschwitz is a space of law, in which violations need to be investigated. His irritation at the fact that Auschwitz is being evacuated at the very moment at which he has collected all the evidence against Rudolf Hess is symptomatic for the absolute destruction of all moral categories (K, 843, 773). In the figure of this judge, one dimension of the instability of Aue's ethical thought and feeling is unfolded. If he is conscious that the National Socialist legal system is only relatively absolute, he implies the absolute relativity of all legal systems. After the war, Konrad Morgen appeared as a witness for the prosecution at Nuremberg: subsequently, he practiced law in Frankfurt, where he died in 1982.

The novel also includes another line of argument, drawing on the ancient conception of law, which Aue himself applies to his actions. The categories of good and evil are to be considered in relation to the deed, and not the will of the person. The criterion for good or bad deeds is the law, as represented in the person of the Führer, who incarnates the will of the people. Hence a crime is not to be attributed to the will of an individual. In the context of the Greek conception of law, Oedipus is guilty because he killed his father, even if he did not mean to. The fact that he deliberately and legally killed a man who had insulted him has no relevance here. From this standpoint, all the Germans are guilty, since they obeyed the Führer as the incarnation of the law that is the product of their collective will. The question, then, is whether they are guilty on the basis of an absolute criterion, or only because the victors have a different system of criteria. Thus "an ordinary man" is not only confronted with the fact that something can be "righteous one day and a crime the next", but with the fragility of law and justice as such. "Who knows where the Law is?" – *La loi, qui sait où elle se trouve?* (K, 593, 546).

The legal question is evoked at the very beginning of the novel, as SS colonel Paul Blobel gives a speech to his men – under the influence of alcohol, but decked out with elements of a speech of Himmler from the 6th of October 1943 in Posnan – in which he declares that in Germany "the Jewish question was to be resolved, fully resolved, without excesses and in a manner in keeping with the requirements of humanity". This, however, was not always able to be ensured in the mass shootings in the East. In practice, women and children cannot be fed after the execution of the men and so: "To include them in our actions, along with their husbands and sons, is in fact the most humane solution given the circumstances" (K, 101, 99-100). The question of the "firm, well-reasoned acceptance of the recourse to violence to resolve the most varied social problems" is that of the role of violence in law and as the ground of the law (K, 670, 616). The notorious sentence of Himmler in his Posnan speech of the 4th of October, 1943 – Aue places his own reflections in the context of the two speeches of Himmler (K, 664-672) – makes clear the connection between crime and law in the concept of decency in an uncanny way.

"I also want to speak to you here, in complete frankness, of a really grave chapter. Amongst ourselves, for once, it shall be said quite openly, but all the same we will never speak about it in public [...]. I am referring here to the evacuation of the Jews, the extermination of the Jewish people. This is one of the things that is easily said: 'The Jewish people are going to be exterminated,' that's what every Party member says, 'sure, it's in our program, elimination of the Jews, extermination – it'll be done.' And then they all come along, the 80 million worthy Germans, and each one has his one decent Jew. Of course, the others are swine, but this one, he is a first-rate Jew. Of all those who talk like that, not one has seen it happen, not one has had to go through with it. Most of you men know what it is like to see 100 corpses side by side, or 500 or 1,000. To have stood fast through this and – except for cases of human weakness – to have stayed decent, that has made us hard. This is an unwritten and never-to-be-written page of glory in our history […] We had the moral right, we had the duty towards our people, to destroy this people that wanted to destroy us […] All in all, however, we can say that we have carried out this most difficult of tasks in a spirit of love for our people. And we have suffered no harm to our inner being, our soul, our character."[49]

If force/violence is a structural moment of the law and its institutionalization, then the extent to which it is applied is a question of quantity, not one of principle. From Hegel to Max Aue, this necessity is justified (as a sacrifice): from Rousseau to Derrida it is seen as a problem. The sophistic figures of argument deployed by Henri Sorge in *The Most High* bring law and transgression into a necessary constellation: the construction of the novel works to the same effect, and reveals the devastating effects of this essential force/violence – civil war and paranoia. The no less sophistic arguments of Max Aue, giving a theoretical foundation to the war and the politics of National Socialism, further untangle this knot. The destruction of the European Jews is the uncanny reality of this secret constitution of law and right, state and politics: such seems to be the conceptual truth of Littell's novel.

The discussion of questions of ethics and of the categorical imperative during an evening at Eichmann's apartment transposes this complex into the sphere of the philosophy of right. During his work on his dissertation in law, Aue had discovered his "love for Kant" and had also been "conscientiously boning up on Hegel and idealist philosophy" (67, 69). He counters Eichmann's doubts on the validity of the categorical imperative with regard to the enemy and particularly with regard to the extermination of the Jews with an argument which bears on the legal-philosophical content of the novel. The Führer is the agent of the law: the Führer's will is the final ground of the law. Aue refers to "the well-known principle *Führerworte haben Gesetzeskraft*" (K, 566, 522): he has himself heard this principle stated by Blobel: "I remind you that *Führerworte haben Gesetzeskraft*, the Führer's word has the force of law" (K, 101, 100). For Aue, these sentences at that moment "weren't much use", because he has the intention of reasoning for himself. But he feels "that [Blobel's] will was holding us and wouldn't let us go, just as other wills had held him" (K, 102, 100). He also finds the argument plausible: "if the supreme value is the *Volk*, the people to which one belongs, and if the will of this *Volk* is embodied in a leader, then in fact, *Führerworte haben Gesetzeskraft*". In carrying the order, and comprehending it in oneself, one becomes a "living Law" (K, 102, 101).

Blobel's speech and the reflections that Aue develops in response prefigure the discussion at the evening at Eichmann's, which leads into general and fundamental principles. Under the condition of the *Führerstaat*, the categorical imperative becomes to act in such a way that one's acts could be approved by the *Führer*. This is accomplished

[49] Himmler's speech before senior SS officers Posnan, Oct 4, 1943. See: Internationaler Militärgerichtshof Nürnberg (IMT): *Der Prozess gegen die Hauptkriegsverbrecher vor dem Internationalen Militärgerichtshof Nürnberg 14. November 1945 – 1. Oktober 1946*. München, Delphin Verlag, 1989, Band 29: *Amtlicher Text. Deutsche Ausgabe. Urkunden und anderes Beweismaterial. Nr. 1850-PS bis Nummer 2233-PS* (Nachdruck der Ausgabe von 1948), p. 145-146.
Documents on the Holocaust, Selected Sources on the Destruction of the Jews of Germany and Austria, Poland and the Soviet Union, Jerusalem, Yad Vashem, 1981, Document no.161. pp. 344-345.

when any given particular will is made into the will of the Führer, such that the will of the individual, as the will of the Führer, makes up the "foundation of the *Volksrecht*". Through any individual, the will of the Führer becomes the general will of the people, because the Führer wants exactly the same thing as the people – and this latter is no abstract quantity, but "something concrete and inalienable: the *Volk*, whose collective will is expressed by the Führer who represents it". Subordination to the will of the *Führer* is, in the end, subordination to the will of the *Volk* which the *Führer* incorporates. This also applies to "most painful tasks"."If our will is to serve our Führer and our Volk, then, by definition, we are also bearers of the principle of the law of the *Volk*, as it is expressed by the Führer or derived from his will" (K, 567, 522).

The corrosion of law and justice is developed still further in another of Aue's reflections. The history of the victors conceals the crimes that led to the victory; such acts become war-crimes when they are committed by the losing side. Aue justifies the German crimes as necessary to the settlement policy, referring back to the Greek conception of the divine principle of necessity. The German colonization of the East is no different from that of the English in India or of the Belgians in Africa; America, too, was not "virgin territory"; "but the Americans succeeded where we failed, which makes all the difference" (K, 590, 542). "And maybe in the end our efforts would have been applauded", since it is "a mistake" to think that "the moral sense of the Western powers differs so fundamentally from our own; after all, a great power is a great power, it doesn't become one by chance, and doesn't remain one by chance, either" (K, 668, 615). This line of argument justifies injustice by recourse to necessity. And necessity has its ground in the will of the people, which asserts itself through force/violence and through war.

In the *Groundwork to the Metaphysics of Morals*, Kant, too, develops the question of ethics in relation to the will, which he understands as based on reason, and thus determines ethics as a *Critique of Practical Reason.*[50] The reasonable will, as the good will, is the practical side of reason. It does not exist for the sake of something else; "it is good through its willing alone – that is, good in itself". If the good belongs to its concept, the result seems to be a tautology. The good will wills the good. The object of the will belongs to the essence of the will itself. The good is the point upon which the will is articulated. The question, then, is how the good is to be appropriately determined. The good will is ground by reference to reason, since reason has its "highest practical function the establishment of a good will" (GMM, BA 5-8, 62-64). The good will acts together with reason, and is finally grounded in reason. It is not good "in itself" but through reason, which is its principle.

[50] Immanuel Kant: *Grundlegung zur Metaphysik der Sitten*, in: *Werke in zehn Bänden*, hg. von Wilhelm Weischedel, Bd. VI: *Schriften zur Ethik und Religionsphilosophie*. Erster Teil, Darmstadt, Wissenschaftliche Buchgesellschaft, 1975, p. 7–102. / *Groundwork of the Metaphysic of Morals*, translated by H.J. Paton. New York: Harper Torchbooks, 1964.
Immanuel Kant: *Kritik der praktischen Vernunft*, in: *Werke in zehn Bänden*, hg. von Wilhelm Weischedel, Bd. VI: *Schriften zur Ethik und Religionsphilosophie.* Erster Teil, Darmstadt, Wissenschaftliche Buchgesellschaft, 1975, p. 103–302. / *Critique of Practical Reason*, translated by Lewis White Beck. New York: MacMillan, 1993.
The texts are cited in parenthesis with the abbreviation GMM and CPR; the first number refers to the German original, the second to the English translation.

An action is not guided by a particular purpose, but the maxim, the "principle of the will" itself, the good, is the motive and the ground for the action. This maxim, as the principle of willing, has metaphysical (a priori, in principle) precedence over the will. The maxim is the subjective principle of the will: the law is its objective principle. The subjective and objective principles would be identical if the reason had "full control over the faculty of desire" (GMM, BA15, 69). The conditional clause indicates that this is not the case, and so the law is only to be obeyed out of "duty", with "full control over the faculty of desire". This is why Hamann, in a letter to Herder (14.4.1785) mocked this good will, as well as pure reason, as a chimera and an idol.

Since the will, as good will, cannot be determined by particular purposes, it must be determined by the "conformity of actions to universal law as such" (*Groundwork* 70). When this conformity forms the principle of the will, I can will that my subjective maxim should be a universal law. The relation of the individual will and the universal law is the center of this problematic. The law is the objective configuration of the will, which, for its part, gives reality to the law GMM, BA 17, 69-70). This universal lies "in the Idea of a reason which determines the will by *a priori* grounds" (GMM, BA 28, 76). In its accordance with reason, the pure will is a "holy" will, finally even a "divine" will, for which the ethical obligation and the will are one and the same (GMM, BA 39, 81). It is absolutely subject to the law. The "prototype" of the will is not the individual will, but the general will, formatted by the form of the law. This is the idealist reversal of Rousseau's conception.

The universal is a final objective purpose, which itself is not a means to any other purpose: rational beings as persons, whose totality makes up humanity. The imperative, then, is to act such that the humanity of each person is always considered as an end, never as a means. Humanity as an end in itself is "the supreme limiting condition of every man's freedom of action". It gives rise to "the idea of the will of every rational being as a will which makes universal law", and thereby "the will's own enactment of universal law" (GMM, BA 65-71, 95-99). The will is subordinate to the law because it has given itself this law on the basis of rational insight. This is the self-legislation of the will. It is will only as this universal. If this is not the case, then reason has to compel the evasive will by duty.

The idea of the will of all rational beings is that of humanity as the instance of the law. The general will has its origin in the idea of humanity. Self-legislation becomes possible, when humanity as the universal molds my selfhood. Humanity and the self coincide in "the will's own enactment of universal law" because the will is rational. The self is the other as humanity. Through the unity of reason, humanity is formed in all individuals, giving rise to "the unity of the form of will" (GMM, BA 80, 104). The conflict of the particular and the universal is always already resolved in the idea of humanity.

The universal law itself cannot be derived from some other source: it is given as idea, and serves as a principle, in order to determine freedom and, with it, the moral law as such. It is presupposed as something in which all individuals must "take an interest" with a view to a successful co-habitation (GMM, BA 102, 117). The freedom of all rational beings leads to the concept of the ethical law, which, conversely, is grounded in the freedom of all rational beings. This is evidently a *petitio principii*. Kant dissolves this "begging the question" through two "standpoints". As a cause, the individual is freedom: as an effect, he or she is law. As a sensory being, he or she is affected: as a rational being, he or she is self-determining. The difference between sensibility and reason, between the passivity of affect and self-determination, dissolves the circle.

Duty is the agent of the violence of the law. In the *Critique of Practical Reason*, Kant addresses a long apostrophe to "Duty! Thou sublime and mighty name" (CPR, A 156, 90). Duty is the prosopopoetic allegory of the law. Its form is the typic. It articulates the two worlds of the human: the affective sensibility of the particular person and the rationally constituted universal personality. The share in the other world is the share of each individual in humanity. By virtue of this share in humanity, the individual person can never be a means to an end, but remains always a "purpose in himself". This follows from the concept of freedom as the essence of personality. Freedom is not a psychological concept that would be derived from the "nature of the soul"; it is a transcendental principle, following from the rational constitution of the human, and allowing us to conceive of the human as free from the sensory world. Freedom, then, is defined as freedom from the sensory world; hence it is essentially rational. Freedom is the positing of reason: thus it can ground the law. Therefore, the law is a nominalistic construction. This is first and last, as in the *Groundwork to the Metaphysics of Morals*, a *petitio principii*. Freedom, humanity and law ground each other reciprocally in the field of the rational constitution of man. This is why duty is a "name", even if a "sublime and mighty" name.

Starting from this line of thought, Max Aue provides Eichmann with a justification for the ethical validity of his acts and for the lawfulness of the National Socialist politics of extermination. It is not the nature of the act that counts, but the fact that it is carried out purely from duty, in accord with the law, as dictated by the Führer. The commands of the Führer are not a mere form, however: they imply a concrete demand for a concrete action: the extermination of the Jews. If such action is to be justified by the final purpose of ethical action, the universality of such action needs to be determined in a different way. The Germans and the Aryan race take the place of rationality and humanity.

The imperative, then, is to act in such a way that the Aryan race as an end becomes "the supreme limiting condition of every German's freedom of action". Thus there is "the Idea of the will of every German as a will which makes universal law", with "its own enactment of universal law". The will is subjugated to the law because it is a law that it has given itself, on the basis of a fully rational consciousness. This is its self-legislation. It is will only when it exists on this plane of universality.

The idea of the will of all Germans is that of the nation (*das Volk*) as the instance of the law. The general will stems from the idea of the nation. Self-legislation becomes possible when nation and race raise the self into the element of universality. Nation and self coincide in their "own enactment of universal law". The self is the other as the nation. It is shaped by the unity of the race in all Germans, and gives "the unity of the form of will". The conflict of individual and universal is overcome in the common element of the nation and the race. Aue's line of thought draws its persuasive power from the scientific justification of the universal, which is only stronger in that Kant himself made the final ground of his argumentation into the positing of a *petitio principii*. With the scientific doctrine of race, the universal is determined anew as nation and race, and for the first time, really justified.

The question, now, is if Aue's argument is a sophistical and illusory version of the logic developed by Kant and Hegel in order to overcome the division of right and law, recognized by Rousseau, or if it is its perverse clarification. The racial-biologically conceived nation takes the place of humanity, as the instance of the universal. If the categorical imperative demands purely formally that every action should be submitted to the maxim of the universal law, then the question has to be that of the criterion for the universality of the law. For Kant and Hegel, this is humanity, whose ground is the universal possession of reason. For Aue, it is the will of the Führer, which has issued from the common will of the nation. The will of the Führer as law is the expression of a self-relational, autopoetic system, just as is the "other world" of the intelligible in Kant, which as "begging the question" takes its origin from a circular justification of freedom through the rational law and of the rational law through freedom, and forms the "totality of rational beings" . To the extent that the Derridean deconstruction of right reveals this constitution of right and law as impossible to dialectically resolve, deconstruction is in fact justice. Thus the schizoid and paranoid ground of the law is made evident. If there is a new treaty, a new decree made by the general will, what is law today can become illegal tomorrow – and vice versa. *La loi, qui sait où elle se trouve?* – "Who knows where the law is?" (K 593, 546). *"'Où est la loi, que fait la loi?* – Where is the law? What does it do?' These screams now were terrible" (MH, 228, 219).

State-crimes can be committed because the law is based in the will, and is therefore antinomically constituted. The "nature of state-crime" lies in the freedom of the will, which is not necessarily oriented by the universality of reason, and is able to choose for itself the object of desire. The demand that its choice should be able to be binding for all can be fulfilled by positing a universal for the will. Its representative is the Führer, whose word has legal force. Such a will – which wants territorial expansion and the elimination of the enemy – can rationally justify its universal validity by invoking the scientific knowledge of racial biology which, with its differentiation between the higher and the lower races, the *Übermenschen* and the *Untermenschen*, the supermen and the subhumans, shows the category of the unity of humanity to be unfounded. The detailed linguistic discussion in the novel traces this line of thought further. If reason is the criterion of the unity of humanity, and language is the organon of reason, this unity is undone by the scientific proof of essential differences between the languages, since this proof implies differences within reason and within humanity. Such sophisms seem to have their origin in the constitution of the will, whose decisions are essentially occasional and determined on criteria of one's own choice. Littell's novel shows the uncanny abyss that opens up with the doubling of the will. This is what has to be understood, if one is to grasp "the nature of state-crime". It is grounded in the two natures of man, as individual and as citizen, which bring about the elementary division of the will in him.

In his interrogation in Jerusalem in 1961, the historical Eichmann also appealed to the "conception of legality at the time", for which the word and the decree of the Führer had legal force. "The final solution of the Jewish question itself – I now refer for example to the special task that was assigned to Heydrich – to put it for once quite blatantly – the killing – was not a law of the Reich – it was an order of the Fuehrer, a so-called Fuehrer's order, and Himmler, Heydrich and the Chief of the Administrative-Economic Head Office divide up amongst themselves, as heads of the offices, [the implementation of] this order of the Fuehrer. In accordance with the legal conception of that time, which was commonly accepted, let us say that the words of the Fuehrer had the force of law."[51] Littell, in conversation with Pierre Nora, summarizes Ian Kershaw's interpretation in a trenchant formulation: "Kershaw describes the National Socialist system as a bureaucracy magnetized by a charismatic Führer. Everyone is thinking about the Führer in his work, and asserts himself in the internal bureaucratic struggles as in line with the will of the Führer [...]. The Jewish problem only has priority for all, because it has priority for the Führer."[52] Ian Kershaw cites Roland Freisler, the President of the national court, who said that it was necessary to judge "as the Führer himself would judge the case".[53]

In *Eichmann in Jerusalem*, Hannah Arendt recalls that the legal force of the Führer's word was "the absolute center of the present legal order" (24). In evidence, she cites Hans Frank's "New Formulation of the 'Categorical Imperative in the Third Reich'" in *Die Technik des Staates* (1942). "Act in such a way that the Führer, if he knew your action, would approve of it" (136; see K 567, 522). For her, the "most difficult moral problem" posed by the trial of Eichmann is "that an average, 'normal' person [...] should be completely incapable of telling right from wrong". This incapacity was indeed "'normal', not an exception: something like a 'normal feeling' was precisely the exception" (26). When she comes back to the legal force of the Führer's word in discussing Eichmann's appeal, Arendt names this split between law and justice – which cannot be resolved by the "unequivocal voice of conscience" – "the central moral, legal and political problem of our century" (148).

The juristic problem posed by the trial of Eichmann is that he was a mass-murderer "who had never killed (and who in this particular instance probably did not even have the guts to do so)" (215). This makes a difference to the concept of murder. Eichmann – and tendentially Aue – is a mass-murderer, without having himself committed murder: an administrative apparatus, by which the mass-murder was organized, stands between him and the genocide. The juristic problem here is the attribution of an act. Can an administrative official who implements a policy and brings it about that certain actions take place, without carrying them out himself, be held responsible and brought to justice for these events? This is the "very essence of this crime, which was no ordinary crime, and the very nature of this criminal, who was no ordinary criminal" and who, in Eichmann's own words, was guilty only of "aiding and abetting" and did not himself murder (246). Anyone could have committed the act in his place, and probably would have done.

The juristic problem posed by the judgment of the Germans in general and of Eichmann in particular is that they were not acting outside of the law, like pirates, but in the name of a state whose "order was criminal", whose laws those such as Eichmann "carried out to the letter". "The juristic problem of all of these trials consists precisely in the

[51] *The Trial of Adolf Eichmann*, Session 11, part 2, available as part of *The Nizkor Project*: http://www.nizkor.org/hweb/people/e/eichmann-adolf/transcripts/
See Hannah Arendt: *Eichmann in Jerusalem: A Report on the Banality of Evil.* Revised enlarged edition. New York, Penguin, 1994, p. 148.

[52] Jonathan Littell / Pierre Nora: *Conversation sur l'histoire et le roman*, in: *Le Débat* 144 (2007), p. 35. Further on this book is cited in parenthesis by page-number.

[53] Ian Kershaw: *Hitler 1936-1945 Nemesis*, London, Allen Lane, 2000, p. 688.

fact that the crimes being tried were committed under conditions in which crime was legal, and every humane action was illegal". The "problem of legalities that stand in the way of justice" (266) is that Eichmann's acts were legal crimes within the law, and as such, put in question the justice of the law itself.

In *Legality and Legitimacy* (1932), Carl Schmitt argued that this conflict was responsible for the "collapse" of the Weimar Republic.[54] Legality is the model for the "legislative state", to which he opposes the "governmental state". This latter "finds its characteristic expression in the exalted personal will and authoritative command of a ruling head of state" (5). His will, which is "in conformity with the law", gives the law its force (6). The "legislative state" takes over its legality-principle from the "governmental state", from the princely absolutism of the pre-modern period, which takes its legitimacy from the tradition of divine right. The "legislative state" transforms the "lawful will" of the ruler into the normativity of the law, to which it thereby gives "the dignity of legality" (10). But this only works as long as "the belief in the rationality and ideality of its normativism is still vibrant" (11), and the laws accord with general ideas (12). However, since the "will of the state" and the "will of the nation" are identical in a "law-state", the consequence is that "every expression of the people's will", and that means "the momentary will of the people present at that time, that is to say, in practical terms, the will of a transient majority of the voting citizenry" (24), becomes law. This leads finally to the alternative between "recognition of the substantive characteristics and capacities of the German people or retention and extension of functionalist value neutrality with a fiction of an indiscriminate equal chance for all contents, aspirations and currents" (94).

Soon after this, Schmitt saw Hitler as the guarantee for the former side of the alternative: his notorious article of 1934 is entitled "The Führer protects the law". In his speech of the 3rd of October1933 at the German Jurists conference, Hitler emphasized the "distinction between substantive law, inseparable from neither morality nor justice and the empty legality of a false neutrality".[55] Schmitt's own thoughts in *Legality and Legitimation* may have thus been given consecration from the highest authority, but there nonetheless remains something of the disrepute of "begging the question" about it. From the experiences of history, the "collapse of the year 1918", the Führer draws "the right and the power to found a new state and a new order":"in the moment of danger, he by the virtue of his domain as Führer, and as the supreme legal authority, directly creates law" (64). The legal force of the Führer's word "springs from the same source of law from which springs the law of every *Volk*. [...] All law stems from the *Volk's right to exist*. Every legal statute, every judicial decision only contains justice insofar as it flows from this source of law" (65).

The will "in conformity with the law" of the Führer is not modelled on the divine will, like that of the absolute ruler of pre-modern states, nor on the absolute Idea, as in Hegel: such instances preserve the general will and its decrees from the arbitrariness of majority decision. It is based on the "*Volk's* right to exist". This implies a perversion of

[54] Carl Schmitt: *Legality and Legitimacy*, translated by Jeffrey Seitzer, Durham, Duke UP, 1994. This book is cited in parenthesis by page-number.

[55] Carl Schmitt: *The Führer Protects the Law*, in: *The Third Reich Sourcebook*, edited by Anson Rabinach and Sander L. Gilman, Berkeley, University of California Press, 2013, p. 63.

the principle of legitimacy; the general will becomes the will of the people, "the momentary will of the people present at that time" and its "right to exist" becomes law and right, protected by the Führer.

Hannah Arendt saw the specificity of the extermination of the Jews, the "true horror of Auschwitz", not in the legalized discrimination, nor in the expulsion of the Jews – there were many precedents for such things – but in the plan "to make the entire Jewish people disappear from the face of the earth", excluding them from the human community and denying them "human status". The "crime against humanity" in the strong sense consisted in this denial of humanity to the Jews. It is a crime against the "very nature of mankind", because it puts in question the unity of the human race (*Eichmann in Jerusalem*, 268). This crime against humanity is uncanny because it was able to be justified with the means of reason, which traditionally grounded precisely the unity of humanity, by methodical science, in the domain of academic research. The specificity of the crime of "the new administrative mass-murderers" is that they have "violated the order of mankind, and not because they killed millions of people" (272). The difference between murder and genocide is not one of quantity, but of quality. This qualitative leap, which first of all consists in denying a certain group the status of human beings by redefining the "very nature of mankind", founds a new norm and a new reality: the essence of man is no longer understood as reason, spirit or soul, but as a physiological reality – and more recently, as a complex structure of circuits in the brain. The spark of the soul has turned into the firing of the synapses.

Since this qualitative leap poses the question of evil, the "new type of criminal" (276) is the enemy of mankind – *hostis generis humani* – as the devil in the Christian tradition was designated. The administrative apparatus becomes the mask of the devil, who appears in the guise of a functionary. What is unique about this constellation is that the administrative order makes it "well-nigh impossible for him to know or to feel that he is doing wrong" (276). Administration is a figure of the collective unconscious and of the *volonté générale* in the modern age. The discrepancy between the act and the consciousness of the act and its consequences is structural in nature. The coordination of the individual and the apparatus confuses and jumbles all the conceptual differentiations needed for a moral judgment: it is "diabolical" in the literal sense of the word. The attempt to understand this is "a long course in human wickedness": what it teaches is "fearsome banality of evil" (252). Such a diagnosis is by no means a minimization: it opens up a perspective upon an uncanny structure.

Littell's character, Max Aue, obliquely confirms this diagnosis. It is true that he disputes that Eichmann was the "enemy of mankind" or "the incarnation of banality", but he then adds a comment that confirms Hannah Arendt's analysis. He refers to Eichmann as "a very talented bureaucrat, extremely competent at his functions":"as a middle manager, he would have been the pride of any European firm" (K, 569-570, 524-525). Eichmann is the incarnation of the type that Aue becomes after the murder of his mother. Aue's reflections therefore can serve as an explanation and a justification for Eichmann too. The new evil exemplified in the attitude of Aue-Eichmann-Morgen, which sets the "enemy of the mankind" into action, is the banality of bureaucratic administration. The psychic deep-structure of the Orestes myth in Aue gives this banal evil a complexity that makes it uncanny, in the Freudian sense of the term.

Aue writes off his discussion as a mere improvisation. He has lost the sense for "such questions" and their "great significance". A "feeling of great indifference" has taken hold of him since the death of his mother, and has allowed him to become entirely absorbed in his work: "Only my work engaged me; I felt I had been offered a stimulating challenge that would call on all my abilities, and I wanted to succeed" (K, 525-526, 571). This feeling also extends to his thought: his ideas on the legal force of the Führer's commands are themselves an effect of this apathy: it is the ethos that is based in apathy. The Auschwitz complex that is subsequently developed can be understood as a consequence of the apathy and the indifference which is produced by the collapse of the familial affect-structure.

To the defeat of Germany in the war, the breakdown of political structures and the destruction of the country, corresponds in Aue the definitive dismantling of the father-imago. The destruction of the fatherland and the father-image triggers a new phase of personality-dissociation. This is the period in which he is pursued by the policemen, Clemens and Weser, and in which the air-raids of the allies are intensified, the American troops land in Normandy, and the signs of defeat become increasingly clear: "the successful landings in Normandy, the surrender of Cherbourg, the loss of Monte Cassino, and the debacle at Sebastopol at the end of May" and "the terrible Soviet breakthrough in Byelorussia" (K, 803, 737).

The dissociation of his personality is triggered when he receives a photograph of his father in the post, showing him as a Freikorps officer in Latvian Courland: "his oval, miniscule face was completely indistinct, unrecognizable" (K, 804, 737). The reaction to the photograph is correlated to the "end-of-the-world landscape" of destroyed Berlin: "of half of the surrounding buildings, only empty silent façades remained, or piles of rubble" (K, 804, 739). The photograph frightens him because he does not recognize his father. In the first place, this is due to the poor quality of the image: "I didn't recognize this man whose face, under his helmet was reduced to a white spot, not completely shapeless, you could make out a nose, a mouth, two eyes, but featureless, without distinctive markings, it could have been anyone's face". The fear comes above all from the "unbearable doubt" whether it is really the father at all. The "ambiguous, elusive photograph" does not give any coherent shape to the "fragments of memory" of the father; rather the "white spot" of the face makes the few details he has disappear. "I didn't have a single picture of my father." The real photograph destroys the phantasmatic image; the actual father, whose miserable role as a terrorist Freikorps-fighter becomes clear to him, destroys the illusory "living present" of the memories in him (K, 805, 739-740).

Since Aue was born in 1913, he could only have seen his father on his visits home during the war; after the war, his father was still active in the Freikorps forces and then disappeared forever. Aue effectively grew up without a father; his father is an absence in his life. In the information given to him by his brother-in-law von Üxkull, he appears as the complete opposite to the fantasy father: "a mad animal [...] A man without faith, without limits" (K, 881, 807). If, for Aue and in the conceptual construction of the novel, the fantasy father is the prefiguration of the National Socialist state and of the Führer, the truth of the matter appears in the prehistory of Aue's father. In fact, after the final dissolution of the Freikorps in 1923 as a consequence of the Versailles Treaty, many of these fighters went into the SA and the SS. Himmler was a member of a Freikorps unit. The dissociation of the father figure and of the law that it represents can be understood as the result of the breakdown of civilization, triggered by the First World War.

The phantasm of the father configured Aue's psychic constitution; it was replaced by the political constitution of National Socialism and Führer, who was correlated to the father. In the concluding section of the novel, the parallel between the family romance and the political history continues through the collapse of psychic and political structures. "This, I said to myself, is what the capital of our eternal millenial Reich is reduced to; whatever happens, we won't have enough for the rest of our lives to rebuild" (K, 803, 739). The photograph and the loss of his father-image trigger a reaction of "rage and anguish" in him. He tears the photograph into pieces, and thereby destroys his own self-image. "I had the impression that my face was melting like wax deformed by the heat of my ugliness and hatred [...] nothing held together anymore" (K, 806, 740). In the fever that follows, he sees in a dream the "final catastrophe" (K, 808, 742). The news of the attempt on the life of the Führer on the 20th July belongs to this general and particular dissolution of the state and the person (K, 818, 752-753). It reveals the menace of the inner enemy combining with the destruction being wrought by the external enemy. At the same time, and corresponding to this development, the fever is accompanied by an uncontrollable regression-fantasy: "I bathed in my sweat as in amniotic fluid, and I would have liked birth not to exist" (K, 811, 745). The three days and four nights of the fever, which, like the head-wound in Stalingrad, bring him to the limit of life and death, make up another "dark night" and a turn in his life. This time it is triggered by the dissolution of the father-imago and by the absolute absence of the father and the fatherland. He only reluctantly resigns himself to this loss, and has evidently still not fully accepted it at the moment of writing out his memories. The wild fantasies that he indulges on von Üxkull's property border on the insanity of psychosis; the policemen Clemens and Weser, who continually appear out of nowhere to harass him, could be part of an incipient persecution-complex. The perfidy of the construction lies in the fact that juristic persecution and persecution-fantasy go hand in hand. The impossibility of clearly distinguishing them points to the basic persecutional character of law, which Rousseau recognized as the aporia in the relationship of the individual and the general will.

This fundamental state of persecution and madness originates in his relationship to his parents, which is modelled upon the Orestes myth. The loss of the father and the phantasmatic father-imago of the psychasthenic personality generate a phantasmatic world-image, within which what is other and foreign appears hostile and vindictive. The phantasm of hostility and persecution makes up a *dispositif* which, when unfolded on the macro-political level, leads to war and extermination. The collective father-imago – God, King, Fatherland – had been dissolved in the wake of the Enlightenment and the Revolution. But the *Volk* and the Führer came to take its place, as one sees in Aue's reflections on the categorical imperative.

Aue's demented fantasies while staying on the property of von Üxkull correspond to the scenario of final defeat for Germany. They make up a complex of wish, fantasy and reality, which are indissolubly bound up together in Aue's perceptions and memories. The fantastic elements, which come from his wishes, become realities in the present of the experience and his later memories of them. They are figures from his past, by which he is fixated and which dominate him. They issue from his drive and affect-constitution, and are located in the limit-zone in between perception, memory and fantasy, hallucination and psychotic imagining. "What I remembered? I didn't even know what a memory was any more" (K, 887, 813). In one of these fantasies, his sister asks him if it is because of her that he does not marry Helen. At this point, it becomes clear that he recognizes the connections. He *wants* to hold on to his past and to the infantile wishes of the Oresteian complex. This is why he does not create a complete delusional system – just as fascism contains delusional elements, but is not in the strict sense a delusional system. The fixation on the Oresteian wishes corresponds to his clinging to his National Socialist convictions.

The complex made up of hatred towards the mother and the incestuous bond with the sister makes every relationship with women impossible for Aue. The sister is the object of affective and sexual fascination, which turns into an obsession that binds all sexual and affective energies. She is Una, "the very one I cannot have, the thought of whom never releases me and leaves my head only to seep into my bones, the who will always be there between the world and me" (K, 763, 701). Mandelbrod's assistants – who have such typical German names as Hilde, Heide or Hedwig – are highly educated and beautiful, but they have the empty beauty that one sees on the portraits of Adolf Ziegler, the "master of German pubic hair". Their representative in reality is Christina Söderbaum; other representatives of the same type – Marika Rökk, Maria Milde, Ilse Werner – attend the parties held by Thomas at his house in Wannsee, before the final collapse (K, 836, 767). Helene – who has a Greek name – is the antitype: to make it explicit, she is named Helene Anders. She represents the possibility of another life. "But the past is a thing that, once it has sunk its teeth into your flesh, doesn't let go" (K, 733, 673). With her, "if things would have been different", a normal, everyday life, with wife and children, "simple and natural", would have been possible. "But my life took another turn, and now it was too late". His basic attitude to life, his physical and psychic make-up, prevents it: in his life, "something was broken so early". "It wasn't just the question of my sister; it was vaster than that, it was the entire course of events, the wretchedness of the body and desire, the decisions you make and on which you can't go back, the very meaning you choose to give this thing that's called, perhaps wrongly, your life" (K, 744, 683-684). His mother's name – Héloïse – refers to the complex of love and passion formed in the Middle Ages, and implies also – with the reference to the exemplary love-story of Abelard and Héloïse – that this complex includes a special relationship between passion and castration.

The incestuous relationship to the sister is only one moment, the tip of the iceberg, formed by the Oresteian complex of familial relations. This "sick" drive and affect structure results in the misery of the body and of desire. In the conception of the novel, this predicament represents the psychic deep structure of Fascism. There is a correspondence between a fundamental psychasthenia and political megalomania. The figure of Helene Anders would be an alternative: she represents the possibility of the "healthy" drive and affect structure which is impossible for Max Aue, because the horror of the past has "sunk its teeth into him": there is a similarity with Henri Sorge, who is likewise haunted by "ancient histories". When Aue decides at the end of the novel to drive to Üxküll's property in the north instead of driving to the south to Helene, it becomes clear that he has decided for the past and for his complex, and against resolution (K, 859-864, 788-792).

The stay on Üxküll's estate takes place in a phantasmatic inner reality. "Of the outside world I no longer had the slightest idea. I didn't know what was happening in it" (K, 902, 827). Aue moves back and forth on the border in between the maintenance and the collapse of the external world. His inner life is configured by incest-fantasies. He imagines the dissolution of all limits as a form of absolute freedom, a phantasmatic state in which the world is entirely at his disposal. "I continued wandering in this limitless space where my thought reigned sovereign, making and unmaking forms with an absolute freedom" (K, 907, 831). This resembles to the point of equivocation the "absolute freedom" of artistic creation, and raises the question if and how the delusion-formation of psychosis is to be differentiated from it or from the *unio mystica* and the *coincidentia oppositorum*. Aue's final phantasmatic incest with his sister resembles such states, culminating in "an unending splash of white light": "my eyes finally opened, cleared and saw everything" (K, 908, 832). The erasure of limits reaches the point where his body dissolves and becomes "something nameless that, reflecting itself, gave itself pleasure as if to something identical yet slightly shifted, not opposite to it but merging with it in its oppositions" (K, 909, 833).

The construction is explosive from the linguistic-philosophical point of view, since Aue has replaced the father as the center of the symbolic order with the sister, and with the incestuous relationship with her. This produces a different symbolic order, which is shaped by the phantasmatic father. He stems from the narcissistic fixation, figurally represented by incest with the twin-sister. This phantasmatic order is precarious in the highest degree, and is constantly on the point of dissolving. The wild excesses and the strangulation games of his childhood, which he resumes on Üxküll's estate, are a symptom of this instability: in them, the childhood incest converges with the fantasized incest on the estate (K, 909-912, 833-836). The "girl" is the moment that creates the structure. From self-strangulation, the chain of associations passes to the girl who is hanged in Russia, and who defecates at the moment of death; she corresponds to the sister of his dream, who defecates in her wedding dress on her wedding night. The killing of this girl – "who was in a certain way like my sister" – is the summit of barbarism for Aue, even if it is objectively necessary in the terms of the National Socialist political goal. The instance of structure-formation (which is, in any case, phantasmatic) is thereby destroyed: "such a cruelty had no name, no matter how objectively necessary, it ruined everything, if one could do that, hang a girl like that, then one could do anything, nothing could be assured" (K, 912, 836).

The dissolution of the personal world, through which he becomes "something nameless", and that of the moral world with the barbaric death of the girl, which is a cruelty "without name", are two corresponding moments. The agent that founds this correspondence is the incest with his sister, which is also "nameless": it dissolves symbolic differences and breaks the limits of the fantasy. In the external world, moreover, it corresponds with the real collapse of Germany.

The encounter with the group of child-fighters, who beat the driver Piontek to death, is an allegory of the dissolution of all political, moral and symbolic form. Its real historical ground is the increasing recruitment of adolescents and children towards the end of the war. Like Aue on Üxküll's estate, they occupy a space in between delusional motivation and actual war; they are the most extreme figuration of National Socialism, as incarnated by Aue and represented in the novel. Their figural value becomes apparent when they continue using a radio which is no longer working: the equipment is real, their use of it is phantasmatic. Thomas Hauser takes advantage of the situation, and makes explicit the content of the phantasm. He pretends to be acting under the orders of the Führer, and says that he needs to speak with him. After simulating the call, he gives the earpiece to the leader of the group, who likewise speaks with the Führer. Once again, the Führer appears as the wild configuring instance of a phantasmatic order, at the edge of madness. The encounter with the German military police shortly afterwards forms a pendant to this scene: Max Aue and Thomas Hauser prove their identity here through a real call (K, 942-944, 864-865). The two calls made to legitimate and save themselves – the one delusional, the other real – show that the border between reality and madness has become permeable. The children with their phantasmatic Führer-complex are an allegory of the psychic situation of Aue and of Germany. They reveal that the Oresteian complex is finally an infantile fixation: a psychic state suspended between childhood and maturity, to which the figure of the Führer gives a phantasmatic form of adulthood.

5 Psychosis

A work which seeks to rival the universal forces,
which seeks to reproduce the effect of a world,
a work in combat with lightning.
Maurice Blanchot, *Faux Pas.*

The end of the war and of Hitler's regime was long described and experienced by the Germans, not as a liberation, as in France, but as a collapse.[56] The authority of the law, which had been represented by the Führer, had collapsed. Post-war German social order can be read as the delusional system set up after the collapse of the law. Friedrich Kittler occasionally said that, as long as there is no adequate theory of psychosis, the best reference, in anticipation, is Thomas Pynchon's novel *Gravity's Rainbow*. He also drew upon Schreber's *Memoirs of my Nervous Illness* and Lacan's commentary on this work. Fundamental to Kittler's work is the thesis that the media are mutations of psychotic symptoms – phantasma appearing in reality in the guise of technology, the technological realization of Schreber's "writing systems (*Aufschreibesysteme*)". This is the "fearsome banality" of the uncanny. In this perspective, all the kinds of apparatus which Heidegger had begun to analyse together under the concept of the *Gestell* – the technological apparatus, the bureaucratic apparatus, the state-apparatus – should be understood as versions of the psychotic "influence apparatus" (V. Tausk). The algorithm is the symbolic form of the *Gestell.*

Sigmund Freud's analysis of Schreber's *Memoirs of my Nervous Illness* in his "Psychoanalytic Comments on an Autobiographical Account of a Case of Paranoia" (1911) works on the assumption that "even thought structures so extraordinary as these and so remote from our common modes of thinking are nevertheless derived from the most general and comprehensible impulses of the human mind".[57] Schreber's case shows that

[56] In 1932, Carl Schmitt diagnosed "the collapse of the parliamentary legislative state" and so he consequently threw his support behind Hitler in 1934, who he saw as the guarantor of a legitimate legal system: "The powerful German Empire, founded by Bismarck, collapsed during the World War" because it was abandoned to a "liberal 'constitutional state'". The "moral outrage over the shame of such a collapse has coalesced in Adolf Hitler and has become in him the driving force of a political act"."The Führer reminds us again and again of the collapse of 1918. Our situation today can be determined only from the perspective of that date." See: Carl Schmitt: *Legality and Legitimacy*, translated by Jeffrey Seitzer, Durham, Duke UP, 1994, p. 3, 13 and Carl Schmitt: *The Führer Protects the Law*, in: *The Third Reich Sourcebook*, edited by Anson Rabinach and Sander L. Gilman, Berkeley, University of California Press, 2013, p.63-66.

[57] Sigmund Freud: *Psychoanalytic Comments on an Autobiographical Account of a Case of Paranoia.* in: Sigmund Freud: *The Standard Edition of the Complete Psychological Works of Sigmund Freud, Vol XII (1911-1913) The Case of Schreber, Papers on Technique and other works*, p. 17; further citations by page-number in parenthesis.

the religious delusion – common in psychosis – is a secondary formation, which is preceded by the fantasy of being emasculated and transformed into a woman. His crisis has its origin in a disturbed relationship to sexual difference and an accompanying conflict of desire. The delusion of sexual persecution is "converted" into a "religious delusion of grandeur" (17). His redemptive fantasy re-casts the shame of his female-ness as a historical necessity. The material for Schreber's madness came from ancient Zoroastrianism, with its doctrine of the two principles. The mutation of thought into madness and the transformation of Schreber into a woman are variant forms of the metanoia that traditionally characterizes an ambitious thought, and the corresponding personality – the transformation of consciousness and the conversion from the old to the new man. Plato gave this movement its prototypical form in the parable of the Cave in *The Republic*, and Augustine described it in the conversion scene of his *Confessions.* The conversion re-configures the personality and the thought in its structure and its dynamic, and gives it a new meaning. Hegel conceived of the *Phenomenology of Spirit* as the "science of the experience of consciousness". It describes "the path of the natural consciousness which presses forward to the true knowledge". The "true knowing" originates from the dialectical movement of thought and is seen "to have come about through a reversal of consciousness itself".[58] The question then is where the line is to be drawn between psychotic mutation and philosophical-theological conversion. Schreiber's "conversion" takes place, following Freud, after a "severe spiritual struggle" (30); the alienated desire is reconfigured by the transformation into a woman. Effeminization is not shameful for Schreber, since the "cultivation of femininity" can be considered to be necessary in accordance with the world-order; it founds his special relationship to God.

Freud traces Schreber's madness back to his relationship with his father, and with his older brother, who becomes the representative of his father. The young Schreber identifies with the father and the law of the father. Schreber's identity is based on a homosexual identification with the father, whose memory becomes "sacred" to him after his early death. During his illness, the position occupied by his father is transferred to his doctor, and then finally to God. This means that the homosexual fantasy of feminization, which originated with the identification with the father, can appear as something that is required by the world-order, and be made into an integral part of the redemptive delusion. When the internal authority of the father breaks down, the dissolution of his own inner subjective world is projected outwards in an apocalyptic vision. The Ego breaks off relations with the world, and projects this secession outwards in the fantasy of the collapse of the world. Given that the world that has collapsed is then built up again in the delusional order, Schreber's madness needs to be understood, not as illness – which breaks off relations with the world – but as an attempt at a cure, a reconstruction of the world. "The delusional formation, which we take to be the pathological product, is in reality an attempt at recovery, a process of re-construction". The ill subject creates another, phantasmatic world, which, illusory as it is, is structured in such a way, that "he can once more live in it" (70).

[58] Georg Wilhelm Friedrich Hegel: *Phänomenologie des Geistes* in: Georg Wilhelm Friedrich Hegel: *Werke*, Bd. 3, edited by Eva Moldenhauer und Karl Markus. Michel, Frankfurt a. M., Suhrkamp, 1976 / *Phenomenology of Spirit*, translated by A.V. Miller, Oxford, UP, 1976, p. 72/49, 97/55.

The world of the symbolic, and with it, the Western symbolic system collapsed with "Auschwitz"; and one can wonder if the reconstruction of the world "after Auschwitz" consists of a delusional system, arising out of the collapse of the symbolic system, or whether it represents a genuine symbolic formation. Schreber's *Memoirs* show that one reason for the generation of delusions is inadequate symbolization, an insufficient integration of the position of the father and of "the law". Since "Father Schreber" is a prototypical representative of the "black pedagogy" (Katharina Rutschky) in the bourgeois milieu of the 19th century, the case of Schreber illustrates a more general social-political phenomenon. The theory of psychosis, then, offers a diagnosis of the modern age, a *discours de la méthode de la folie* in the age of universal madness.

"Officialese [Amtssprache] is my only language": thus Arendt cites Eichmann in her *Report on the Banality of Evil*, in order to illustrate his incapacity for genuine speech and thought, his inability "to think from the standpoint of somebody else". "No communication was possible with him, not because he lied but because he was surrounded by the most reliable of all safeguards against the words and the presence of others, and hence against reality itself" (49). This same "horrible" misrepresentation of reality was experienced by the entire republic. Eichmann is the model-figure in whom the attitude of the average German becomes fully visible. Arendt names such an attitude as a "distortion of reality" and illustrates it with statements of the Minister of Defense, Franz Josef Strauβ and the literary critic of the *Rheinischer Merkur* (58). A particularly clear form of this distortion of reality is the testimony of Eichmann's defender, Dr Robert Servatius, who describes the gassing of the Jews as a "medical matter"; in response to interrogation of the judge Halevi, he clarified that a killing is, after all, a "medical matter". Arendt notes that it was "one of the few great [moments] in the whole trial", since it indicated the attitude of the "ordinary German" to acts that "in other countries are called murder" (69).

The parallels between Schreber and Max Aue are evident. The identificatory relation to the father, and the transposition of this identification to the sister, and then to the Führer and the Party that he joins after losing his father and sister; the homosexual element; the conception of salvation through National Socialism – all these aspects are the elements of the psychobiography of Aue, which extends to include hatred of his mother. In the post-war period, after the collapse of the Reich, Aue works in the administration of a medium-sized business. The essential importance of narcissism, underlined by Freud in his analysis, is always evident in Aue, from his erotic activity in front of the mirror to the scene at the end of the novel, where he falls into the river, as he observes his image in the water. While looking at himself in the mirror, he says that he looks for "my true face filling my features from behind, the features of my sister's face" (K, 514, 474). His incestuous relationship to his twin-sister, his wish for a "complete fusion" with her, is oriented towards the realization of narcissistic desire. After his separation from his sister, this desire is transposed into his desire for men. It is decisive for an understanding of his condition that the face of his mother is suddenly interposed "in between these two faces and their complete fusion"; the identificatory relationship with the mother appears behind the desire for his sister. Immediately after this experience, Aue travels to the South, and kills his mother and stepfather (K, 518, 478). Certainly, it would be futile to subject a literary character to psychoanalysis. But the question remains as to how one should understand the parallels between Schreber's redemption-fantasies and Aue's conversion to National Socialism. Does Aue's story show signs of madness in him? Since Aue can be seen as an allegorical figure of National Socialism, this question leads into the center of the fascist complex.

In his analysis of the *Memoirs of my Nervous Illness*, Jacques Lacan observed that Schreber's delusions exhibit essential elements of the subsequent fascist formation.[59] He is part of a more general socio-political syndrome, which develops in the 19th and early 20th century. "The themes that emerge in a second early stage of his delusion are obviously tied to this complex of cultural encirclement which sadly blossomed into the renowned party that was to throw all Europe into war. The encirclement by the Slavs, by the Jews, all this is already there in this worthy fellow" (211, 250).

One of the elements of Lacan's theory of psychosis is the assumption that there are "master signifiers", without which the system of significations would not operate, would not have reality or truth. The transformation of need into desire, of drives and feelings into meaning is a basic characteristic of the human mode of being. The problem then is to identify the agent that articulates this transformation. Language, by means of its differential constitution, is an infinite system of references, in which the signifying process remains open, without a stopping point or a final meaning, due to what Lacan calls the "slippage" of the signifiers. There has to be a regulative instance of articulation if the flow of signs and of the corresponding thoughts are to create meaning. This is the sense of the Oedipal complex. It introduces the instance of the No and the Law of the Father; in this way, it is the condition of the possibility of the symbolic order, considered as an articulated reality and the formation of meaning. The Oedipal complex is the cornerstone of the symbolic order; this stone is laid down in the name of the Father. The psychotic rejects the father, who then turns up as a phantasmatic figure in reality. The result is a delusional system which, for Schreber, takes the form of a salvational fantasy and a writing system.

In Lacan's interpretation, the psychotic identifies with the father in the element of the imaginary, rather than in the symbolic. Schreber's masculinity is not configured symbolically, in the name of the Father, but is modelled on the image of the Father. In consequence, the world that he inhabits is not truly meaningful, but illusory, and his language is imaginary rather than symbolic. The visual image is not transformed into language; language is itself treated like an image. The iconic component of language becomes absolute. One of the symptoms of this condition is the tendency to take words literally. When Hegel, at the beginning of the *Phenomenology of Spirit* finds the pronoun "*mein*" (mine) in the verb *meinen* (to mean or intend) and brings both into a complex train of thought concerning the *Allgemeinen* (the universal), this is a consciously cultivated form of this attitude. Heidegger's etymologizing terminological innovations in *Being and Time*, and even more so, the creations of his linguistic logic in his late work – the *lesende Lege* or the *fugend fügende Fug* – belong in the same field. And the mimologics of Cratylean concepts of language should evidently also be understood as belonging to this imaginary attitude, which takes words literally.

The process by which language as an internal system of differences acquires a referential dynamic is regulated through the Oedipus complex. The "signification of the

[59] Jacques Lacan: *Le Séminaire. Livre III: Les Psychoses*, edited by Jacques-Alain Miller, Paris, Seuil, 1981 / *The Psychoses: the Seminar of Jacques Lacan Book III, 1955-1956*, translated by Russell Grigg, New York, Norton, 1993. The book is cited in parenthesis.

phallus" is a transcendental signified which gives a stopping point to the slippage of the signifiers and the flow of thoughts. This is the systematic location of Derrida's debate with Lacan. The point of contention is whether symbolization is possible without such a transcendental signified. Lacan and psychoanalysis insist upon the necessity of such a configuring agent, which is derived from a mythical configuration. The Oedipal complex configures the symbolic order, and makes it possible for it to constitute reality and not delusion. This is the necessary function of the myth of Oedipus. It structures the subject in such a way as to enable the relation to the world and to other people. Psychoanalysis does not pose the question as to why the family-romance is to be configured specifically by the myth of Oedipus, and not for example, by the myth of Phaeton or that of Orestes. It assumes that the Oedipal configuration is the foundation of Western civilization and its symbolic order. Nonetheless, one can ask how other myths carry out a similar work of configuration, and how these various configurations, which are formally equal in value, generate different world-conceptions. The myths of Orestes and Phaeton are also family-romances. It would be possible, then, to define the dominant myth of a given civilization, and, moreover, to inquire whether myths are indispensable for the configuration of the symbolic order. Lacan names such a configuring agent a "*point de capiton*" – a quilting point. This is the stopping point of the flow of meanings; it signals that from out of which and for the sake of which a symbolic configuration is constituted (281-283, 303-305). Hence we can begin to understand what Littell means when he says that he was first able to bring his collection of historical materials into a configuration through the Orestes myth.

The family-romance is enacted between father, mother and child; therefore the relation between the sexes also plays a role in it. The dominant myth configures the symbolic order in accordance with the configuration of the sexes; the myth creates a grid that regulates the perception of sexual difference. Myth is the agent that facilitates the transition from the imaginary order of the mother into the symbolic order of the father, from the particular to the general, from the private sphere to the public sphere. The wishes and feelings as desire form the flow of meanings, whose dynamic is given a structure by the symbolic order. Language and desire relate to one another as signifier and signified. As the dream has a "navel" in Freud's ingenious figure of thought, "the spot in every dream at which it is unfathomable", so too the symbolic order has a navel, an elementary node at which it is "unfathomable"; this node is formed by the dominant myth.[60] The navel is the trace that remains of the original relation to the mother; it is the representative of the reign of the mothers in the world. If desire is, first and last, desire for the mother, then the meaning of the symbolic order configured through the father-instance is evidently the mother – but the mother as refused or denied.

According to the basic thesis of psychoanalysis, the roles in the family romance are configured by the Oedipus complex. Personality is an intersubjective process – it is the symbolic and internalized drama of these psychic functions. The Oedipally configured symbolic order constitutes the reality and the conception of the world proper to man. The human is inherently Oedipal. The solution to the riddle of the sphinx is "man". Oedipus is the one who solves this riddle. Therefore he is the figure of man as such. The

60 Sigmund Freud: *The Interpretation of Dreams*, in: Sigmund Freud: *The Standard Edition of the Complete Psychological Works of Sigmund Freud. Vols IV and V*, p. 549.

Oedipal complex towers over the individual and the ego; it is the super-ego in the elementary sense, the truth of the meaning of the paternal No and of the Law, which it is the task of the myth to configure. The psychotic lacks this basic configuring agent. Thus his conception of the world, formed in the element of the imaginary, breaks down in the moment of crisis. In the case of Schreber, this takes place as he is about to take over the paternal position within the law – as he becomes director of the state court at Chemnitz and Senate President of the High Court in Dresden. One can ask then if this mythic structure and the law that it is configured by it is an artificial and conventional construct. Or does the myth of Oedipus have an essential and foundational significance – might it even make possible significance in the true sense? The question here is that of the role of myths as symbolic configuring agents.

At essential moments, the Orestes myth is the reversal of the Oedipus myth. Orestes has a mortal hatred of his mother and idolizes his father. Melanie Klein in her "Reflections on the Oresteia" conceives of the Orestes complex as an "inverted Oedipal complex" (286). Orestes idealizes his father; he denies the father's brutal conduct as a warrior in sacrificing his own daughter, Iphigenia, and identifies himself with the idealized father. What is decisive then, is whether the paternal instance of the law that is instituted on the Aeropagus at the end of the *Oresteia* in fact succeeds in transfiguring this idolized father into a truly symbolic paternal function; or if it merely makes the idolized law into the order of the polis. It is not Orestes who configures this structure; it is Athena who institutes the law. When she decides in favor of Apollo that the maternal order is subordinate and that matricide does not have to be expiated, the paternal function that is thus instituted is idolic, in the sense that it does not integrate the order of the mother into the law instituted in the name of the father. It rejects the maternal order, replacing it with the idolic father, instead of symbolically transforming it into the law.

At the beginning of the *Oresteia*, in *Agamemnon*, the Chorus recalls the sacrifice of Iphigenia by her father, Agamemnon, who was driven by "all too impassioned passion" (*orga periorgos*), giving this out as what was right (*themis*); his "uttermost audacity" (*pantótolmon*) over-ruled his prudent mind (*phronein*) (v. 215-221). By contrast, the Chorus refers to Clytemnestra's report on the fire-beacon after the victory over Troy and her warning to the victors as prudent and well-meaning (*sophron' euphronos*); she speaks like a man (v. 351).

The Chorus conceives of the action of the play within a horizon marked out by the elementary opposition of light and darkness. It calls upon the representatives of these powers, Zeus and the Night: "Hail, sovereign Zeus, and you, kindly Night" (*o Zeu basileu kai nyx philía*). If the balance of these powers is disturbed by guilt (v. 389), it is a problem both for the city (v. 395) and for the cosmos (356). With the image of the judicial ballot, Agamemnon underlines that the transgression of the law of hospitality and the adultery which took place with the seduction of Helen represented a clear injustice, and that the triumphant war against Troy was therefore just. In that situation, the gods cast their ballots unanimously for the Greeks (v. 813-817). The difference is marked with the legal situation at the end of *The Eumenides*. The solution to the fundamental conflict of the *Oresteia* is by no means so clear, as is shown by the equal ballots cast for each side.

The *Oresteia* shows that it is purely a sovereign decision, deeply arbitrary and unjust, that resolves the legacy of the "primal sin" (*protarchon aten*, *Agamemnon* 1190), the cycle of crime and expiation, the aporia of the double *Dike* and the antinomic constitution of the law. At the end of the play, Athena – who has no mother, who is her father's child – institutes the law in the Greek polis by fiat in the name of the father. The *Oresteia* shows the conventional and ideological nature of this paternal order of the polis, of the law, and of the political order. Hence the arguments that are opposed during the trial are so "biting and pointed", in the manner of a sophistic agon.[61] The play also shows that the decision is ultimately made in the name of Apollo. After the murder of his mother, Orestes invokes his father – "not mine, but he who surveys all this, the Sun"– to testify before the court that he has "justly" (*endíkos*) killed his mother (*Libation Bearers*, v. 984-989). The new law in the name of the father is instituted in the spirit of the light and rational moderation; limits are placed on the Erinyes, the Night, and the measureless *orgè*, which led Agamemnon to sacrifice his daughter, Iphigenia. The solution of Athena, the goddess of rational insight, is a moment of what Freud called "progress in intellectuality"; it is linked to the position of the father, to monotheism and to the law that is made in the name of the father. When Orestes justifies matricide at the end of *The Libation Bearers*, however, through Apollo, from whom he received "the spells that gave me the audacity for this deed" (*philtra tolmès*, v. 1026-1031), it is implied that his excessive *tolma* is in no way different from that of Agamemnon, when he ordained the killing of Iphigenia. The act becomes just only through the imposition of the law.

The archaic agon between the maternal order and the law of the father, represented in the trial on the Areopagus by the conflict between Erinyes and Apollo, corresponds to the relation between the imaginary and the symbolic, in Lacan's conception of the psychic dynamic. Conflict is a fundamental element of the human constitution, and of the political order corresponding to it. It could form one moment in the structure of the law, which Derrida analysed in terms of the antinomy of justice and force/violence. "You learn to be patient and you discover how long history – even if it is ended – really is, and how slowly it passes. It's like a dream" (MH, 133 / 130).

The *Oresteia* links this conflict with sexual difference, dramatizing it in divisions between man and woman, husband and wife, father and mother. The difference of the sexes plays out on a shared ground. In *The Libation Bearers,* the Chorus opposes "man's overweening spirit" (*hypértolmon an-/ dros phrónema*) and the "reckless passions of women" (*gynaikon [...] pan-/ tólmous érotas*). The phronetic and the erotic determinations converge in the spirit of *tolma*, a word signifying risk and audacity. The hubris of reckless daring is linked with guilt (*á -/ taisi synnómos*). It has its ground in "loveless love" (*apérotos éros*), that is, in a conflict within the erotic itself (v. 594-601).

The Eumenides begins at the Delphic oracle, the site of the "the first prophet, Earth" (v. 2). The *omphalos*, the navel of the earth (v. 40; 166), is the point at which the cosmic order opens on to "the unfathomable". The genealogy of the prophetess in the oracle informs us that Gaia was replaced by Themis, the figure of justice in the age of the Titans; and Themis then succeeded by her sister Phoebe, the grandmother of Apollo. Thus the Oracle ultimately passes from the order of Gaia to the order of Apollo. The Pythian oracle is therefore entirely aligned with Apollo, with Athena, and in this line, with the Olympian Zeus, "the most high" (*hýpsiston*) (v. 19-29). The genealogy of the

[61] Karl Reinhardt: *Aischylos als Regisseur und Theologe*, Bern, Francke, 1949, p. 151.

priestesses brings out the articulation between the archaic maternal order and the new law, in which the father takes precedence. Apollo is "the spokesman of Zeus, his father" (v. 19). Themis – or Justice – is the point of articulation between the maternal order and the law of the father; and this law, in order to be truly just, has to forge a link with the "unfathomable", the navel of the earth. This is precisely what is at issue in the trial of Orestes.

This other side of the law and justice has feminine and maternal connotations. In the Eumenides, its representatives are the Erinyes, "this extraordinary band of women" who brood "black, altogether disgusting" (*bdelýktropoi*) next to Orestes (v. 46-52).[62] Apollo's characterization of the Erinyes is nothing but denigration and vilification. They are "loathsome maidens" whom one would like to spit at (*katápystoi korai*), "creatures hateful (*misémat*) to the men and to the Olympian gods" (v. 67-73). The Erinyes are figures of hatred and fear in relation to the mother. Apollo is the center of this elemental misometry and metrophobia. The constellation made up of the dark chthonic deities and the light Olympians reappears in the form of the oppositions between Clytemnestra and Agamemnon, and between the Erinyes and Apollo. After Apollo's encouraging speech to Orestes, the shade of Clytemnestra, therefore, exhorts the Erinyes to fulfil their duty. In this way, the elemental constellation of the conflict is dramaturgically represented upon the stage. Orestes is the figure in whom this conflict is enacted. The action, as Karl Reinhardt argues, is "played out within the soul" and is "to be seen at the same time as a division in the divine order".[63]

Once Orestes and the Erinyes have set forth their respective arguments, Athena recognizes that they each have an equal legal claim, and concedes that she cannot decide on the verdict (v. 470-481). As a solution she proposes to have a court made up of jurymen with witnesses and presentations of evidence. The conflict is thus referred to the human jurisdiction of the judiciary of Areopagus. Apollo's evidence carries misometry to the point of denying the part of the mother in human reproduction. He argues that the woman is only the host of the male seed; the generative power lies with the man. As proof, he refers to the birth of Athena from the head of Zeus, without contribution of any mother (v. 658-666). Athena is the mythical figure of the phantasm of motherlessness.

62 The field of words around "the disgusting" – *bdelygma*, *bdelyktos*, *bdellytto* – is sonically close to the verb *bdallo* – to suck, to milk, from which *bdella* – the leech is derived. The reference to the Erinyes as *bdelýktropoi* may then be a subtle pun with a pseudo-etymological background. A model for this literalization of words is the explanation of the name Helen in *Agamemnon*; she is named thus because she is *helénaus*, *hélandros*, *heléptolis* – ship-destroying, man-destroying and city-destroying (v. 687-690). The bdelyktropic Erinyes are then figures of the hostile mother, of the persecuting breast that sucks blood instead of giving milk. The image of the sucking breast is explicitly introduced in *The Libation-Bearers*. When the Chorus tells Orestes of Clytemnestra's dream that she gave birth to a serpent which lacerates her breast as it suckles, he identifies with the serpent, which "drew in clotted blood with the beloved milk" (*philón gala*; v. 523-540). And Clytemnestra shows Orestes her breast, before he kills her, recalling "the milk that nourished you" (*eutráphes gala*; v. 896-898). Littell takes up this motif, in developing the ambivalent relation of Max Aue to his mother and to his mother's breast.

63 Karl Reinhardt: *Aischylos als Regisseur und Theologe*, Bern, Francke, 1949, p. 135.

The trial is the primal scene of the Areopagus as a legal institution, and as such, it is the myth of the origin of law in Greece. Athena links the name Areopagus – the Hill of Ares – with the triumph of Theseus over the Amazons at this precise location. The site of Greek law is originally the site of the triumph over the Amazons, representing an order of women. Thus, as Christian Meier underlines, in the political realm, the men "have the whole say and women none".[64] In making her decision, Athena, the daughter of her father, explicitly invokes her motherlessness. When the ballot is tied, it is her vote that decides (v. 734-743). She transforms the resentful Erinyes into kindly Eumenides, giving them responsibility for the sowing of seeds and for cattle, while she herself takes over the protection of warriors. In this way, she lays the foundation for the opposition of two moments of civilization: on the one hand, an interior and domestic order, associated with femininity, and on the other hand, an outward turned order of agriculture and war, associated with masculinity. And yet the question remains if this transformation of the order of the mother into the law of the father is a moment of truth or of delusion.

[64] Christian Meier, *The Political Art of Greek Tragedy*. Trans. Andrew Webber. Baltimore: Johns Hopkins University Press, 1993, p. 134.

BIBLIOGRAPHIE:

Aeschylus: *Oresteia*, translated by Herbert Weir Smyth. London, Heinemann, 1926.

Peter-André Alt: *Kunst des Bösen nach Auschwitz (Adorno, Kertész, Littell)*, in: Peter-André Alt: *Ästhetik des Bösen*, München, Beck, 2010, p.482-511.

Hannah Arendt: *Eichmann in Jerusalem: A Report on the Banality of Evil*. Revised enlarged edition, New York, Penguin, 1994.

Aurélie Barjonet / Liran Razinsky (Eds.): *Writing the Holocaust Today. Critical Perspectives on Jonathan Littell's "The Kindly Ones"*, Amsterdam / New York, Rodopi, 2012.

Georges Bataille: *Giraud – Pastoureau – Benda – Du Moulin de Laplante – Govy*, in: Georges Bataille: *Œuvres complètes*, Vol. XI, Paris, Gallimard, 1988, p. 188-197.

Julien Benda: *La trahison des clercs*, Paris, Grasset, 1975 ([1]1927; [2]1946) / *The Treason of the Intellectuals*, translated by Richard Aldington, New York, Norton, 1969.

Walter Benjamin: *Drei Bücher: Viktor Schklowski: "Sentimentale Reise durch Rußland"; Alfred Polgar, "Ich bin Zeuge"; Julien Benda: "Der Verrat der Intellektuellen"*, in: Walter Benjamin: *Gesammelte Schriften*, Band III: *Kritiken und Rezensionen*, edited by Hella Tiedemann-Bartels, Frankfurt a. M., Suhrkamp, 1972, p. 107-113.

Dietz Bering: *Die Epoche der Intellektuellen 1898–2001. Geburt – Begriff – Grabmal*, Berlin, Berlin UP, 2010.

Christophe Bident: *Blanchot – partenaire invisible. Essai biographique*, Paris, Champ Vallon, 1998.

Maurice Blanchot: *Le mythe d'Oreste*, in: Maurice Blanchot: *Faux pas*, Paris, Gallimard, 1971 ([1]1943), p. 72–78 / Maurice Blanchot: *The myth of Orestes*, in: Maurice Blanchot: *Faux Pas*, translated by Charlotte Mandell, Stanford, UP, 2002, p.59-64.

Maurice Blanchot: *Le Secret de Melville*, in: Maurice Blanchot: *Faux Pas*, Paris, Gallimard, 1971 ([1]1943), 273-277 / *The Secret of Melville*, in: Maurice Blanchot: *Faux Pas*, translated by Charlotte Mandell, Stanford UP, 2002, p. 239-247.

Maurice Blanchot: *Le Très-Haut*, Paris, Gallimard, 1975 ([1]1948) / *The Most High*, translated by Allan Stoekl, Lincoln, University of Nebraska Press, 1996.

Maurice Blanchot: *La folie du jour*, Montpellier, Fata Morgana, 1973; first in: *Empédocle* 1 (1949), p. 13-22 / *The Madness of the Day*, translated by Lydia Davies, Barrytown, Station Hill Press, 1981.

Maurice Blanchot: *L'écriture du désastre*, Paris, Gallimard, 1980 / *The Writing of the Desaster*, translated by Ann Smock, Lincoln, University of Nebraska Press, 1986.

Maurice Blanchot: *The Intellectuals in Question*, in: *The Blanchot Reader*, edited by Michael Holland, London, Blackwell, 1995/ *Les Intellectuels en Question. Ébauche d'une réflexion*, in: *Le Débat* 29 (1984) and Paris, Fourbis, 1996.

Maurice Blanchot: *Ecrits politiques (1958-1993)*, Paris, Editions Lignes-Léo Scheer, 2003.

Karl Heinz Bohrer: *Der Skandal einer Imagination des Bösen. Im Rückblick auf* Die Wohlgesinnten *von Jonathan Littell*, in: *Merkur* 65 (2011) 741, p. 129-146.

Martin Buber: *Gog und Magog. Eine Chronik*, in: *Werke*, Band 3: *Schriften zum Chassidismus*, München / Heidelberg, Kösel / Lambert Schneider, 1963, p. 999-1261.

René Char: *Recherche de la base et du sommet*, in: René Char: *Œuvres complètes*, Paris, Gallimard, p. 625-768.

Jacques Derrida: *Force de loi. Le "Fondement mystique de l'autorité"*, Paris, Galilée, 1994 / *Force of Law, The Cardozo Law Review* 11, 1989-1990, p. 973-1045.

Documents on the Holocaust, Selected Sources on the Destruction of the Jews of Germany and Austria, Poland and the Soviet Union, Yad Vashem, Jerusalem, 1981.

Euripides: *Elektra*, in: Euripides: *Tragödien IV: Elektra, Helena, Iphigenie im Lande der Taurer, Ion*, griech./dt., übersetzt von Dietrich Ebener, Darmstadt, Wissenschaftliche Buchgesellschaft, 1990 ([1]1977 Akademie Verlag Berlin), p. 7-109.

Euripides: *Orestes*, in: Euripides: *Tragödien V: Die Troerinnen, Die Phoenikerinnen, Orestes*, griech./dt., übersetzt von Dietrich Ebener, Darmstadt, Wissenschaftliche Buchgesellschaft, 1990 ([1]1979 Akademie Verlag Berlin), p. 209-313.

Michel Foucault and Maurice Blanchot: *Foucault /* Blanchot, translated by Brian Massumi and Jeffrey Mehlman, Cambridge MA and New York, Zone Books, 1987.

Sigmund Freud: *The Origins of Psychoanalysis: Letters to Wilhelm Fliess. Drafts and Notes: 1887-1902*, translated by Eric Mosbacher and James Strachey, London, Imago, 1954.

Sigmund Freud: *Creative Writers and Daydreaming*, in: *The Standard Edition of the Complete Psychological Works of Sigmund Freud, Vol IX (1906-1908) Jensen's Gradiva and other works*, p. 141-154.

Sigmund Freud. *Psychoanalytic Comments on an Autobiographical Account of a Case of Paranoia.* in: *The Standard Edition of the Complete Psychological Works of Sigmund Freud, Vol XII (1911-1913) The Case of Schreber, Papers on Technique and other works*, p. 1-84.

Sigmund Freud: *New Introductory Lectures on Psychoanalysis*, in: *The Standard Edition of the Complete Psychological Works of Sigmund Freud, Vol XX (1932-1936): New Introductory Lectures on Psychoanalysis and other works*, p. 1-182.

Sigmund Freud: *Family Romances*, in: *The Standard Edition of the Complete Psycho-*

logical Works of Sigmund Freud, Vol IX (1906-1908) Jensen's Gradiva and other works, p. 235-242.

Sigmund Freud: *Medusa's Head*, in: *The Standard Edition of the Complete Psychological Works of Sigmund Freud. Vol XVIII (1920-1922) Beyond the Pleasure Principle and other works*, p. 273-274.

Sigmund Freud: *The Interpretation of Dreams*, in: *The Standard Edition of the Complete Psychological Works of Sigmund Freud. Vols IV and V.*

Andreas Gelhard: *Das Denken des Unmöglichen. Sprache, Tod und Inspiration in den Schriften Maurice Blanchots*, München, Fink, 2005.

Jean Giraudoux: *Elèctre* (1937), in: Jean Giraudoux: *Théâtre complet*, édition de Jacques Body, Paris, Gallimard, 1982, p. 593-686.

Jonas Grethlein: *Littells Orestie. Mythos, Macht und Moral in* Les Bienveillantes, Freiburg, Rombach, 2009.

Georg Wilhelm Friedrich Hegel: *Phänomenologie des Geistes*, in: Georg Wilhelm Friedrich Hegel: *Werke*, Bd. 3, edited by Eva Moldenhauer und Karl Markus. Michel, Frankfurt a. M., Suhrkamp, 1976 / *Phenomenology of Spirit*, translated by A.V. Miller, Oxford, UP, 1976.

Georg Wilhelm Friedrich Hegel: *Grundlinien der Philosophie des Rechts oder Naturrecht und Staatswissenschaft im Grundrisse*, in: Georg Wilhelm Friedrich Hegel: *Werke*, Bd. 7, edited by Eva Moldenhauer and Karl Markus Michel, Frankfurt a. M., Suhrkamp, 1975 / *Elements in the Philosophy of Right*, translated by H.B. Nisbet, Cambridge, UP, 1991.

Martin Hose: *Die Orestie des Aischylos – die Götter, das Recht und die Stadt*, in: Elke Stein-Hölkeskamp / Karl-Joachim Hölkeskamp (Hg.): *Die griechische Welt. Erinnerungsorte der Antike*, München, Beck, 2010, p. 418-434.

Margaret-Anne Hutton: *Jonathan Littell's* Les Bienveillantes*: Ethics, Aesthetics and the Subject of Judgment*, in: *Modern and Contemporary France* 18 (2010), p.1-15.

Internationaler Militärgerichtshof Nürnberg (IMT): *Der Prozess gegen die Hauptkriegsverbrecher vor dem Internationalen Militärgerichtshof Nürnberg 14. November 1945 – 1. Oktober 1946.* München, Delphin Verlag, 1989, Band 29: *Amtlicher Text. Deutsche Ausgabe. Urkunden und anderes Beweismaterial. Nr. 1850-PS bis Nummer 2233-PS* (Reprint of the 1948 edition).

Immanuel Kant: *Grundlegung zur Metaphysik der Sitten*, in: Immanuel Kant: *Werke in zehn Bänden*, edited by Wilhelm Weischedel, Bd. VI: *Schriften zur Ethik und Religionsphilosophie*, Darmstadt, Wissenschaftliche Buchgesellschaft, 1975, p. 7-102. / *Groundwork of the Metaphysic of Morals*, translated by H.J. Paton, New York, Harper Torchbooks, 1964.

Immanuel Kant: *Kritik der praktischen Vernunft*, in: Immanuel Kant: *Werke in zehn Bänden*, edited by Wilhelm Weischedel, Bd. VI: *Schriften zur Ethik und Religionsphilosophie*, Darmstadt, Wissenschaftliche Buchgesellschaft, 1975, p. 103-302. / *Critique of Practical Reason*. Translated by Lewis White Beck. New York: MacMillan, 1993.

Ian Kershaw: *Hitler 1936-1945 Nemesis*. London, Allen Lane, 2000.

Melanie Klein: *Reflections on the Oresteia*, in: *Envy, Gratitude and Other Works 1946-1963*. London, Vintage, 1997, p. 275-300.

Martin von Koppenfels: *Schwarzer Peter. Der Fall Littell, die Leser und die Täter*, Göttingen, Wallstein, 2012.

Jacques Lacan: *Le Séminaire. Livre III: Les Psychoses*, edited by Jacques-Alain Miller, Paris, Seuil, 1981 / *The Psychoses: the Seminar of Jacques Lacan Book III, 1955-1956*, translated by Russell Grigg, New York, Norton, 1993.

Jochen von Lang: *Das Eichmann-Protokoll. Tonbandaufzeichnung der israelischen Verhöre*, Berlin, Severin und Siedler, 1982.

Marc Lemonier: *Les bienveillantes décryptées*, Paris, Pré aux Clercs, 2007.

Jonathan Littell: *Les bienveillantes*, Paris, Gallimard, 2006 / *The Kindly Ones*, translated by Charlotte Mandell, London, Chatto and Windus, 2009.

Jonathan Littell: *Die Wohlgesinnten. Marginalien*, Berlin, Berlin Verlag, 2008.

Jonathan Littell / Pierre Nora: *Conversation sur l'histoire et le roman*, in: *Le Débat* 144 (2007), p. 25-44.

Jonathan Littell / Samuel Blumenfeld: *Il faudra du temps pour expliquer ce succès*, in: *Le Monde des livres* 11 / 17 / 2006.

Jonathan Littell / Jesús Ruiz Mantilla: *Die Nazis hatten Kultur*, in: *Frankfurter Allgemeine Zeitung* 11 / 3 / 2008, S. 37.

Jean François Lyotard: *Tombeau de l'intellectuel*, in: *Le Monde*, 7 / 16 / 1983; also in: Lyotard: *Tombeau de l'intellectuel et autres papiers*, Paris, Galilée, 1984, S. 11-22.

Robert Mantero / Bernard Pingaud: *Ecrivains d'aujourd'hui. 1940–1960*, Paris, Grasset, 1960.

Giuseppina Mecchia: *L'écrivain et la communauté. Maurice Blanchot et la politique de 1932 à 1968*, Princeton, UP, 1997.

Jeffrey Mehlman: *Legacies of Anti-Semitism in France*, Minneapolis, University of Minnesota Press, 1983.

Christian Meier, *The Political Art of Greek Tragedy*, translated by Andrew Webber, Baltimore, Johns Hopkins University Press, 1993.

Hannes Opelz: *The Political Share of Literature. Maurice Blanchot*, 1931-1937, in: *Paragraph. Journal of Modern Critical Theory* 33 (2010) 1, p. 70-89.

Origen: *On the Principles*, translated by Frederick Crombie in: *Anti-Nicene Fathers* Vol. 4, edited by Alexander Roberts et al., Buffalo, Christian Literature Publishing, 1885.

Gerhard Poppenberg: *Ins Ungebundene. Über Literatur nach Blanchot*, Tübingen, Niemeyer, 1993.

Gerhard Poppenberg: *Mit Nachsicht?* in: *PhiN* 1 (1997), p. 69-72.

Gerhard Poppenberg: *Antike oder Moderne? Altes und Neues zum freien Willen*, in: *Philosophische Rundschau* 58 (2012), p. 259-273.

Franz Leopold von Ranke: *Vorrede* zu *Geschichte der romanischen und germanischen Völker* (1824), in: Franz Leopold von Ranke: *Sämmtliche Werke* Band 33/34, Leipzig, Dunckler & Humblot, 1885, p. 7.

Liran Razinsky: *Not the Witness We Wished For. Testimony in Jonathan Littell's "Kindly Ones"*, in: *Modern Language Quarterly* 71 (2010), p. 175-196.

Karl Reinhardt: *Aischylos als Regisseur und Theologe*, Bern, Francke, 1949.

Jean-Jacques Rousseau: *Les rêveries du promeneur solitaire*, in: Jean-Jacques Rousseau: *Œuvres complètes* I, edited by Bernard Gagnebin und Marcel Raymond, Paris, Gallimard, 1959, p. 993-1099.

Jean-Jacques Rousseau: *Du contrat social*, in: Jean-Jacques Rousseau: *Œuvres complètes*, III: *Du contrat social. Ecrits politiques*, edited by Bernard Gagnebin and Marcel Raymond, Paris, Gallimard, 1964 / *Discourse on Political Economy and The Social Contract*, translated by Christopher Betts. Oxford World Classics, 1994.

Gerhard Sälter: *Gerüchte als subversives Medium. Das Gespenst der öffentlichen Meinung und die Pariser Polizei zu Beginn des 18. Jahrhunderts*, in: *Werkstatt Geschichte* 15 (1996), p. 11-19.

Jean-Paul Sartre: *Les mouches*, in: Jean-Paul Sartre: *Théâtre complet*, edited by Michel Contat et al., Paris, Gallimard, 2005, p. 1-87 / *The Flies and In Camera*, translated by Stuart Gilbert, London, Hamish Hamilton, 1946.

Jean Paul Sartre: *Qu'est-ce qu'un collaborateur?*, in: Jean-Paul Sartre: *Situations*, Vol. III, Paris, Gallimard, 1949, p. 43-61.

Carl Schmitt: *The Führer Protects the Law*, in: *The Third Reich Sourcebook*, edited by Anson Rabinach and Sander L. Gilman, Berkeley, University of California Press, 2013.

Carl Schmitt: *Legality and Legitimacy*, translated by Jeffrey Seitzer, Durham, Duke UP, 1994.

Daniel Paul Schreber: *Memoirs of my Nervous Illness*, translated by Ida Macalpine and Richard Hunter, Harvard College, 1955, reprinted by New York Review of Books, 2000.

Susan Rubin Suleiman: *When the Perpetrator Becomes a Reliable Witness of the Holocaust. On Jonathan Littell's "Les bienveillantes"*, in: *New German Critique* 36 (2009) 106, p. 1-19.

The Trial of Adolf Eichmann. The Nizkor Project: http://www.nizkor.org/hweb/people/-e/eichmann-adolf/transcripts/

Steven Ungar: *Scandal & Aftereffect. Blanchot and France since 1930*, Minneapolis, University of Minnesota Press, 1995.